T0240615

A Different Look at Artificial Intelligence

Ulrike Barthelmeß • Ulrich Furbach

A Different Look at Artificial Intelligence

On Tour with Bergson, Proust and Nabokov

Ulrike Barthelmeß
Koblenz, Germany

Ulrich Furbach
Koblenz, Germany

ISBN 978-3-658-38473-9   ISBN 978-3-658-38474-6   (eBook)
https://doi.org/10.1007/978-3-658-38474-6

© The Editor(s) (if applicable) and The Author(s), under exclusive licence to Springer Fachmedien Wiesbaden GmbH, part of Springer Nature 2023
This book is a translation of the original German edition „Künstliche Intelligenz aus ungewohnten Perspektiven" by Barthelmeß, Ulrike, published by Springer Fachmedien Wiesbaden GmbH in 2019. The translation was done with the help of artificial intelligence (machine translation by the service DeepL.com). A subsequent human revision was done primarily in terms of content, so that the book will read stylistically differently from a conventional translation. Springer Nature works continuously to further the development of tools for the production of books and on the related technologies to support the authors.
This work is subject to copyright. All rights are solely and exclusively licensed by the Publisher, whether the whole or part of the material is concerned, specifically the rights of translation, reprinting, reuse of illustrations, recitation, broadcasting, reproduction on microfilms or in any other physical way, and transmission or information storage and retrieval, electronic adaptation, computer software, or by similar or dissimilar methodology now known or hereafter developed.
The use of general descriptive names, registered names, trademarks, service marks, etc. in this publication does not imply, even in the absence of a specific statement, that such names are exempt from the relevant protective laws and regulations and therefore free for general use.
The publisher, the authors, and the editors are safe to assume that the advice and information in this book are believed to be true and accurate at the date of publication. Neither the publisher nor the authors or the editors give a warranty, expressed or implied, with respect to the material contained herein or for any errors or omissions that may have been made. The publisher remains neutral with regard to jurisdictional claims in published maps and institutional affiliations.

This Springer Vieweg imprint is published by the registered company Springer Fachmedien Wiesbaden GmbH, part of Springer Nature.
The registered company address is: Abraham-Lincoln-Str. 46, 65189 Wiesbaden, Germany

Acknowledgements

Some parts of this book were motivated by discussions in lectures and talks on artificial intelligence. The idea of linking the treatment of memory in AI and in literature was inspired by Jonah Lehrer's book *Prousts Madeleine* [1]. We would like to thank Isabelle Barthelmeß, Beate Körner, Claudia Schon and Holger Schultheis for reading and commenting on parts of the book. Special thanks go to Dr. Sabine Kathke, who was extremely helpful and valuable as editor.

Reference

1. Lehrer J (2010) Prousts Madeleine. Piper, München

Contents

1

Introduction

Abstract The importance of computer science and artificial intelligence is explained in this introductory chapter. It is argued that related topics should not only be discussed from the perspective of the natural scientist or technician, but that philosophers, literary figures and artists should also be brought into the discussion.

Technical developments have always influenced and changed our lives. This is probably most clearly illustrated by the example of the steam engine and the subsequent industrial revolution in the 19th and 20th centuries in Europe. The mechanisation of industrial production had not only changed people's working conditions, but also their living conditions. Social structures changed, a rural exodus set in, and the cities in the industrial areas offered unhealthy and inhumane living conditions, at least for the working class.

Computer science, has shaped our life and work in a similarly drastic way. When I started studying computer science in the early 1970s, I always had to give an explanation when I was asked about my field of study: Informatik (the German word for computer science), that is, computers and stuff... At that time, computers were used at most in large companies that could afford the immense acquisition or leasing costs of the so-called mainframe computers. The first PC did not appear on the market until the 1980s, and with it the image of computer science in society gradually changed. Suddenly it was possible to communicate using computers, airline ticket sales were handled via computer networks, database systems permeated public administration, and

© The Author(s), under exclusive license to Springer Fachmedien Wiesbaden GmbH, part of Springer Nature 2023
U. Barthelmeß, U. Furbach, *A Different Look at Artificial Intelligence*,
https://doi.org/10.1007/978-3-658-38474-6_1

we slowly learned how to use this technology. In companies, employees had to make friends with the "colleague computer", microprocessors found their way into our automobiles and improved comfort. Not quite so noticed by the public, computers at the same time became more and more important for the armament industry and thus also for our security. In the meantime, information technology has permeated our entire working and living environment. Very slowly, relatively unspectacularly, but no less drastically, we are becoming dependent on computer systems and networks in pretty much all areas of life. The Internet is, so to speak, the lifeline of our society. Learning, knowledge acquisition, finance or consumption are no longer imaginable without the worldwide internet. At the same time we have also become more transparent. The search engine, social network or shipping platform operators know more and more about us, about our buying and living habits. User data has become an important economic asset; companies that have access to large amounts of user data achieve huge market values, entire business models are based on this customer data. This data is interesting because it can be analysed using techniques developed in the field of artificial intelligence (AI) research, so that a wide range of conclusions can be drawn about people who generate this data. Of course, this information can also be used to make our lives more convenient: My online retailer knows which products I prefer and sends me special offers accordingly, my personal assistant in my smartphone or in the speaker box in my living room knows what my taste in music is and makes appropriate suggestions.

These AI techniques are different from the algorithms we use in computer science. Of course, these are also algorithms, computer programs developed by humans, but these programs have the ability to learn. This means that they evolve and modify themselves as they are used – the direction this takes depends on the data the processes encounter as they are used. In the case of these so-called machine learning (ML) methods, it is not possible to foresee in detail from the outset how they will evolve. ML techniques in particular have recently given AI research and development an immense boost: AI systems win quiz shows, they beat world-class players in highly complex games such as Go, they help make our vehicles safer by assisting drivers in a variety of ways, and they are even starting to make vehicles drive autonomously. AI systems are also being used to make military weapons systems intelligent and possibly even autonomous – the implications for deployment and the impact on military and political decisions are seen by many AI researchers as highly critical and dangerous. To this end, there is a call to outlaw autonomous lethal weapons worldwide, which has already been signed by thousands of scientists and well-known companies.[1]

We live and work with computer systems that behave intelligently or even are intelligent. These systems can make decisions and evolve on their own. Some researchers even predict AI systems that could become smarter and more powerful than humans and possibly subdue humanity. These are by no means just some science fiction fans, but serious scientists and public figures. Whatever one thinks about it and whichever the direction the discussion takes, we have the impression that many arguments are more emotional than technically based when questions like "Can machines be intelligent, can they have emotions or consciousness, can they outperform us humans?" are discussed.

Are these all questions that can only be answered with the help of a sound technical and scientific education? Should we leave the discussion about these socially relevant questions to scientists alone?

We think that we all should deal with these questions and with the aftermath of AI. In contrast to Schwanitz in [1], we do not want to limit education to the humanities and the arts. Education certainly also includes a certain understanding of scientific contexts. Only then can we really understand which developments affect and change our society. This is actually obvious – since time immemorial, humanities scholars, philosophers and literary figures, but also visual artists have been using and discussing new scientific findings in their work and thinking them further. We will refer to the fact that Marcel Proust writes at great length about memory and remembering, Vladimir Nabokov deals with remembering and time, and Henri Bergson works on the relationship between body, mind and consciousness. And we refer to the neuroscientist and Nobel Prize winner Eric Kandel, who also describes the influences of the natural sciences on artists and painters in Vienna at the beginning of the twentieth century.

In the following, we would like to discuss some of these works from the humanities, literature, and philosophy and relate their topics to issues and methods from AI research. By linking scientific and engineering methods with discussions from the arts and cultural studies, we hope to make a small contribution to the understanding of the profound social change that accompanies the spread of AI technologies. But perhaps this will also allow AI practitioners to understand that questions they are investigating are also relevant and being investigated in completely different fields.

---

[1] https://autonomousweapons.org

The selection of AI techniques presented here is by no means exhaustive. We have concentrated on topics from our own research areas, such as logical reasoning, knowledge and memory. We have added topics that have recently become particularly relevant in AI research, such as machine learning and artificial neural networks.

The same applies to the themes and techniques from the arts and humanities. We have engaged with authors and scholars whose subject matter is human beings, their physicality and their consciousness. The focus was on the question of what constitutes memory and thinking, what role our emotions play when we move as human beings in life, in the world, when we as artists exhaust the possibilities to design new original ways of seeing ourselves and the world.

The temptation to draw on science fiction literature to discuss parallels with scientific developments is of course very great. And it would certainly be exciting to pursue corresponding scientific-technical speculations. However, we have refrained from doing so, as this would go beyond the scope of our investigation, since we are not interested here in discussing possible consequences of possible developments in a distant future with their social and moral implications. We are interested in the extent to which such seemingly remote fields as AI, art and philosophy reveal a kinship. Perhaps AI can even benefit from insights from the humanities, similar to modern technology, where clever solutions are copied from nature under the heading of bionics?

Structure of the book In the next chapter, the research field of AI is characterized so that individual techniques or methods of AI can then be explained in the following chapters and related to approaches from philosophy and art. Furthermore, in individual chapters we deal with topics such as creativity, free will, consciousness and language. The chapters can, but need not, be read in chronological order. References to content are indicated by appropriate chapter references. However, reading the following chapter on artificial intelligence would be helpful in understanding what follows. Some of the chapters begin with freely associated thoughts that may help to set the mood for the topic – they are printed in italics in each case.

Reference

1. Schwanitz D (1999) Bildung. Eichborn Verlag, Frankfurt a.M

2

Artificial Intelligence

Abstract Unfortunately, a universal definition of artificial intelligence does not exist. We use an essay by computer pioneer Alan Turing to illuminate the term, and we describe various tests to evaluate artificial intelligence. Finally, we outline the state of the art of the research field.

In this section we want to characterize the research field of artificial intelligence (AI). In different textbooks one can find different descriptions or actually circumscriptions of the field. The problem is simply that it seems strange to define artificial intelligence when already the term intelligence is not clearly defined. Such a situation is not at all uncommon – we often operate with terms for which we have no clear and unambiguous definition. Take concepts like happiness or consciousness, for which countless studies and debates exist; even a concept like pornography is not clearly definable, although it even plays a role in legislation and jurisprudence. Similarly with intelligence – we use the term, we even have various tests that measure something like intelligence, but we do not manage to get a clear definition.

2.1 What Is Artificial Intelligence?

Instead of now giving an overview of the many attempts to define the terms intelligence and AI, we will go back to an essay from 1950, when computer development was still in its infancy. This may seem strange, considering the immense progress that computer science and AI research have made since then.

© The Author(s), under exclusive license to Springer Fachmedien Wiesbaden GmbH, part of Springer Nature 2023
U. Barthelmeß, U. Furbach, *A Different Look at Artificial Intelligence*,
https://doi.org/10.1007/978-3-658-38474-6_2

The essay we want to discuss here is entitled "Computing machinery and intelligence" and is by Alan Turing [1]. With remarkable foresight, this pioneer was able to foresee and discuss the development of AI and its implications even back then. I stumbled across this 1950 title while I was looking for a dissertation topic. This was 1977 – I had been looking into theoretical computer science for my dissertation. Turing is well known to computer scientists worldwide for his outstanding contributions to theoretical foundations of computer science and also mathematics. For the general public, and especially for the British, he stands for the decoding of the cipher machine Enigma, which was used by the German Wehrmacht in World War II. More about the person can be found in the following box.[1]

Alan Turing, born in London in 1912

and died in Wilmslow, Cheshire, in 1954. Turing was studying mathematics at a time when the foundations of several novel disciplines in the natural sciences were being laid. Einstein is publishing his work on relativity, the logician Kurt Gödel has just published his landmark paper which shatters David Hilbert's dream of the complete formulability of mathematics, and various mathematicians are beginning to think about the notion of computability. With his simple yet powerful (thought) machine, later named the Turing machine after him, Turing presents an instrument for the analysis of algorithms and computer programs that is still in use today (see Chap. 3).

During the Second World War, Turing works on the decryption of German radio messages. At Bletchley Park, he is a member of a military unit that has set itself the goal of cracking the German ENIGMA encryption machine. In fact, Turing contributes significantly to the success of this enterprise.

From 1948 onwards, Turing turned increasingly to the development of programmable digital computers. The paper on artificial intelligence [1] is written during his time at the University of Manchester, where Turing is involved in the development of the Manchester Mark I. Turing also writes the programming manual for this machine, which contains numerous programs, mostly arithmetic functions written in a simple programming language.

Prior to his work on deciphering the Enigma, Turing spent several years at Princeton, where he studied under Alonzo Church and also received his doctorate in 1938. There is evidence from this period that Turing was concerned with concepts such as creativity and intuition in connection with Gödel's incompleteness result. For example, already in his dissertation [3] he presented logics which leave room for mathematical intuition; in a separate section he discusses the role of intuition and ingenuity in seeking formal proofs. We will discuss this problem in detail in Chap. 7; in the meantime it is known that emotions also play a decisive role in intelligent reasoning.

---

[1] Much of the exposition in this section is taken from a paper published by one of the authors in a computer science journal on the occasion of Turing Year [2].

(continued)

The work of that period can be understood as a direct continuation of the ideas of the great philosophers of the Enlightenment. In Chap. 3, we address the view of Descartes in our treatment of the mind-body problem. In connection with the notion of AI, the work of Gottfried Wilhelm Leibniz from the eighteenth century is also important. Leibniz had, among other things, designed mechanical calculating machines and developed the idea of being able to build future machines that could solve problems in mathematics and philosophy on their own. In the future, philosophers would not "dwell" on argumentation, they would simply say "calculemus" – "let us calculate". For a detailed discussion of the road leading from Leibniz through Frege, Cantor, Hilbert and Gödel to Turing, see [4]. Against this background it is not at all surprising that Turing already at that time dealt with the question whether machines can think.

Turing is sentenced to prison for homosexuality in 1952. Faced with a choice, he opts for medical treatment with hormones. Probably as a result of this therapy he falls ill with depression and dies by suicide in 1954.

Alan Turing is now considered an outstanding computer science pioneer whose work is still ubiquitous in modern computing. In 2013, he was officially rehabilitated by the British government.

Can machines think? – Alan Turing asks this question in the first sentence of his article [1]. For most computer scientists in the 1970s, thinking machines were not yet a topic of discussion – amazing that someone had already started thinking about intelligent machines years before the famous Dartmouth Conference (1956), which is considered the "cradle of artificial intelligence". When you look at the state of the art in digital computing from that time, Alan Turing's essay is incredibly visionary.

In this article, Turing argues for the ability of machines to be intelligent and, more importantly, in it he proposes a kind of test that can be used to check whether a machine is behaving intelligently. Using this essay as a guide, the following section will explain what we can think of as the field of artificial intelligence research. We closely follow Turing's essay by largely sticking to its structure, reproducing his arguments and relating them to modern AI developments.

2.2 The Imitation Game

Turing proposes an imitation game to show whether a computer is intelligent. In the meantime, this game is called the Turing Test:

Let us imagine a room with two persons, A is male, and B is female. A questioner of any gender is in another room from which he can communicate in writing with A and B without seeing them.

The object of the game for the questioner is now to determine which of the two persons is the man and which is the woman. The role of person B, i.e. the woman, is to help the questioner; Turing suggests that this is best done if she tells the truth. Person A, on the other hand, must try to deceive the questioner with his answers. Turing now replaces person A in this game with a machine and asks the question whether in this configuration of the game the questioner is deceived as often as in the version without a machine. He understands this question as a refined version of the original question "Can machines think?"

In the first version of the imitation game, in which all parts are still taken over by humans, the gender of the persons involved plays a decisive role. In further discussion, Turing finally arrives at a version of the imitation game in which Part A is taken over by the computer and Part B by a man and both have to pretend to be a woman (Fig. 2.1, left). Meanwhile, in the literature, the following version is called the "Turing test" (Fig. 2.1, right). The game is played between a machine A, a human B, and an inquirer C. The goal of the game is to find out which of the two is a human. C is to find out which of the two conversation partners A or B is a human.

This Turing test is thus based on the hypothesis that the computer should deceive the questioner in such a way that the latter mistakenly believes it to be

Fig. 2.1 Imitation game. Left: Computer and man, both above the line, pretend to be a woman. The questioner below the line is to find out which of the two is a man or a woman. Right: Computer and man pretend to be a man, the questioner below the line has to find out which of them is a man

a human being. Of course, this is a view of intelligence that is very much oriented towards verbal behavior. This immediately offers some criticisms, which Turing also addresses directly – we will take this up below.

2.3 The Computer

In a detailed section, Turing explains what he means by a digital computer, and in particular one that is to take on the role of the machine in the imitation game. Considering that the common usage at the time was such that the term computer was thought of as a human being performing computations, it is not surprising that Turing thoroughly explains what kind of computer he has in mind here. He describes the architecture of a digital computer, which consists of memory, arithmetic unit, and a control unit. He goes into detail about the program control of such a computer, commenting also that the control of machines could also contain an element of chance, whereby such machines could even be said to have a kind of free will (see Chap. 8).

In a separate section, Turing explains that the digital computer, as he described it, is a "discrete state machine", but at the same time universal in character. Any other new machine that one comes up with to perform certain computations is (in principle) unnecessary; the same computation can be performed by a suitably programmed digital computer.

Thus Turing formulates the imitation game more precisely by asking, "Is there a digital computer that can satisfactorily play the role of the machine in the imitation game?" He also immediately answers the question in the affirmative. According to him, in 50 years it will be possible to program computers to master the game in such a way that an average interviewer will have no more than a 70% probability of recognizing the machine after five minutes of questioning. Now this prediction didn't come true – but that's quite often the way with prophecies. Turing's statement that by then the general opinion will have changed in such a way that one will then not expect any contradiction when talking about thinking machines, seems more important.

After Turing has succinctly formulated his opinion, he goes into detail about various counter-arguments to his thesis. We will discuss some of them in the following; before that, however, we will take a look at a competition that closely follows the Turing test.

In 1991, Hugh Gene Loebner offered a $100,000 prize to the first program to pass the Turing test. Since then, there has been an annual Loebner competition in which programs attempt to fool a human interrogator exactly as Turing required. Each year, $2000 is awarded to the program that manages to fool the most judges. Here, however, it is admitted that the subject of the conversation is severely limited. It is doubtful whether this contest advances the field of AI; the only certainty is that chatbot developers[2] keep coming up with new techniques to fool the contest's interviewers. Marvin Minsky, one of the doyens of AI, saw the Loebner Prize as an "odious and unproductive annual publicity campaign" and offered $100 in prize money to anyone who could stop Loebner from running this contest. Loebner responded by arguing that the first winner of the contest, i.e., the $100,000 winner, must finish the contest and thus receive the additional $100 from Minsky. Consequently, he argues, Minsky is now a co-sponsor of Loebner's prize.

2.4   Turing's Objections

Theology and Head in the Sand

Turing now discusses and refutes some of the possible objections in his paper. He briefly addresses a possible theological objection, namely when it is argued that God has given an immortal soul to humans, but not to animals and machines. Turing refutes the argument by concluding that God could also give a soul to elephants, since he is omnipotent; but he could just as easily allow machines to have a soul. And anyway, if one thinks of Galileo, one can get the suspicion that in the past these kinds of arguments were doubtful.

Turing also briefly addresses the head-in-the-sand argument: The consequences of thinking machines are terrible. Therefore, one must hope and believe that machines cannot think. Although Turing did not consider this argument worthy of further discussion, it is worth addressing. Indeed, if we apply it to robots, especially androids, we can very often hear objections of this kind to the development and use of human-like robots. In science fiction literature in particular, robots are often portrayed as threatening; they threaten individual humans (as in "Terminator", for example) or are even a danger to the whole of humanity (in "Matrix", for example). Well-known, of course, are Asimov's laws, which robots would have to obey in order not to harm humans.

By his own admission, Asimov found the "Frankenstein pattern" that robot stories generally followed at the time boring; he first postulated the three laws of robotics in his story "Runaround" [5]:

---

[2] Chatbot: a combination of "to chat" and "robot".

1. A robot must not injure a human being or cause harm through inaction.
2. A robot must obey the commands of a human unless such commands conflict with the first law.
3. A robot must protect its own existence as long as that protection does not contradict the first or second law.

He demanded that robots must be constructed in such a way that they must obey the laws, that they cannot do otherwise at all. Of course, his demand can also be translated to mean that robots simply must not develop a consciousness of their own. These robot laws are the subject of numerous science fiction narratives and films, very often addressing the paradoxes that can arise in the application of the laws. In [6] we have discussed in detail the reasons for this view. Religious aspects, influenced by our European Christian tradition, can play a role; but also basic psychological reasons can be given for the head-in-the-sand argument.

It is interesting to note that there are cultural differences in dealing with robots. In large parts of Asia, for example, one can observe a much more casual approach to robots than is the case in our Christian culture. The reason for this could perhaps lie in the soul – Asian religions usually have an animistic view of the world, according to which not only people but also all other things in nature are animated. It is then no further step to regard robots as animate and thus as equal (for more details see [6, 7]).

Mathematics

Turing argues that mathematicians could argue that since Gödel it is clear that the power of machines, i.e. digital computers (even with infinite memory), is limited.

There are questions that cannot be properly answered yes or no. From this one could deduce that this inability makes the machine inferior to the human intellect. Turing now argues that, on the one hand, it is not at all clear that freedom from error is a necessity for intelligence and that, after all, humans also make mistakes and give wrong answers and are nevertheless sometimes classified as intelligent.

Consciousness

Even before the publication of Turing's essay, there were numerous discussions about thinking machines; for example, Wiener's book on cybernetics had already appeared in 1950, and the work of McCulloch and others on learning in neural networks was also well-known. Turing's starting point in this section on consciousness is a 1949 paper by Geoffrey Jefferson, which postulates that machines can only think if they have consciousness. Turing counters that the only way to really know if a machine is thinking would be to be that machine itself. In philosophy, such an approach would be called solipsism: One can only be certain about one's own consciousness – no consciousness exists outside of one's own. The same argument would apply, however, to the question of the consciousness of other people, though such a solipsistic approach is usually not applied to people. – Why then with machines?

Certainly the concepts of intelligence and consciousness are related; we will deal with them in more detail in Chap. 11.

Learning

The keyword learning plays an important role in connection with intelligence. In one section, Turing addresses an argument that one hears quite often – even today – when trying to explain to a layman what the goals of AI research are: "Surely a computer can only execute what you have programmed into it beforehand". Lady Lovelace was certainly one of the first to formulate this. She is known among computer scientists for having probably written the first computer program for Charles Babbage's "Analytical Engine". In 1843 she translated a description of the Analytical Engine from French and added numerous notes to this translation, which also contain several passages in which she emphasizes that the machine cannot think. Explicitly she formulates that the machine can only execute what we know how to describe. Turing goes into detail about Ada Lovelace, including the argument that machines can learn. Turing describes how we could design learning procedures based on the development and learning process of a child. He describes procedures that we call "reinforcement learning" in AI and that are now being used very successfully in complex intelligent systems (see also Sect. 5.5). Turing also makes comparisons here with evolutionary procedures – he even talks about how sensible and important it is to introduce random elements into development and learning. We now know that this is necessary for the convergence of machine learning when genetic methods are used.

2.5 Turing and Nouvelle AI

Turing also mentions that learning machines are limited in terms of their actuators and sensors, and that therefore instructions to the machine would have to be of a more intellectual nature. At the end of his article, Turing expresses the hope that machines will be able to compete with humans in all purely intellectual areas. The difficulty here is which tasks to choose for this purpose; should one limit oneself to abstract activities such as playing chess, or should one equip machines with the best possible sensors and teach them language?

In fact, this has been an important strategy for the development of intelligent systems for many years: take a sophisticated and efficient piece of machinery, add a few sensors at most, and let it try to solve an "intellectual task". Examples include playing chess, understanding natural language texts, image analysis, or theorem proving. We have seen spectacular success in many of these areas, and of course there are other interesting and challenging tasks in these subfields of AI. Nonetheless, since the late 1980s, a view has been established that was then labeled "Nouvelle AI".

Instead of relying exclusively on the thinking machine to develop intelligent systems, biological evolution is now being taken as an example. One first tries to teach artificial systems movement, reaction and all that is necessary for survival. Only then are reasoning, problem solving, language and expert knowledge tackled. We take up this view again in Chap. 3 on body and mind.

2.6 The Chinese Room

From a philosophical point of view, however, there remains the question of qualia, the subjective and conscious internal mental states of a system. Can a machine have such conscious states? A much-cited counter-argument is "Searle's Chinese Room" [8]: an English-speaking human is in a locked room full of boxes of Chinese characters. The person does not understand Chinese, but has an extensive set of rules for converting Chinese character sequences into other Chinese character sequences. The person now receives a sequence of characters without knowing that it is a question in Chinese. She manipulates the sequence using the set of rules and transmits the result to the outside world, where it is understood as an answer to the question. The person, however, did not understand either the question asked in Chinese or the generated answer. According to Searl, it is therefore impossible to construct an under-standing, thinking system by means of symbol-manipulating rules.

In a purely functionalist view, on the other hand, one would attribute the ability to understand Chinese to the entire system, i.e. the unit consisting of the room, the person and the set of rules.

However, according to Block [9], one can also extend the thought experi-ment as follows: He obliges all inhabitants of China and assumes that every-one has a telephone and a list of numbers that he must ring after his telephone has rung. No message is transmitted, there is only the call – the analogy to a neural network with a predetermined connection structure is obvious. If one now declares certain Chinese as "inputs" and others as "outputs", one can enter coded questions and finally read a coded answer from the outputs after a spread of all ringing signals. Again, no single one of the persons can have understood what it is all about.

Taking up the analogy of the neural network again, a person would corre-spond to a single neuron in the network of the brain. This raises the question of whether I expect any of the individual neurons of my brain to understand the lines I am writing ... We will discuss questions around qualia and con-sciousness in Chap. 11.

In this context, the European Flagship Project HBP – The Human Brain Project – should also be mentioned.[3] The aim of a large European interdisci-plinary consortium is to produce a simulation of the entire human brain. This would provide us with a model that would allow us to investigate countless questions from the neurosciences, cognitive research or even philosophy.

2.7   Alternative Turing Tests

Turing's imitation game to answer the question of whether machines can think has now led to fruitful and exciting discussions for over 60 years. Of course, numerous extensions and modifications of the test have been pro-posed. In the review article [10] some of them are explained. One extension that takes into account the discussion about nouvelle AI is the total Turing test (TTT). Here it is required that the machine not only responds to verbal input, but also has sensorimotor capabilities, i.e. is a robot. This test can be intensified to the total total Turing test (TTTT) if one demands that the arti-ficial brain is not only functionally indistinguishable from the human brain, but also resembles it on a neuromolecular level. Those who reject this

---

[3] http://www.humanbrainproject.eu, accessed October 2018.

requirement as too chauvinistic can also choose the variant TTT*, where instead of neuromolecular similarity, indistinguishability with respect to the mode of action (flowchart match) is required.

Other variants of the Turing test try to exclude by their design that architectures can exist by means of finite automata. For example, the "sphere test" requires that the machine wins an infinite number of rounds of the test, which of course cannot be achieved with a finite automaton.

The TRTTT (truly total Turing test) makes the reference to evolution: before robots are allowed to take part in a test like the Turing test, they must have evolved as a "race". They must have invented their own language or games such as chess. Only when this stage of development has occurred are individual specimens allowed to participate in the test. Of course, one could also imagine that these robots would in turn build artificial systems that would evolve themselves again to pass the TRTTT, which would in turn make them ...

Finally, a variant of the Turing test should be mentioned, which you have certainly already undergone. In order to distinguish computer programs from humans, the CAPTCHA technique is used on many websites. In the visual variant, the viewer is asked to interpret an image and enter the result textually into an input mask. CAPTCHA is the acronym for "Completely Automated Public Turing Test to Tell Computers and Humans Apart".

2.8 Status of AI

Now that we have talked in detail about the nature, sense and nonsense of artificial intelligence, this section will outline the state of the field as it stands today.[4] We will use examples to show that AI has already penetrated deep into areas of our daily lives. Whereas the successes from the 1980s were very often in artificial and unrealistic environments, today we find AI techniques in solutions to extremely complex problems. We will discuss "Deep Question Answering", autonomous vehicles, mathematics and the Chinese board game Go in the following.

Deep Question Answering

In Deep Question Answering (DQA), the task is to understand and answer a question formulated in natural language. In this process, given pieces of text

---

[4] Parts of this section can also be found in [11].

are not to be examined for the occurrence of key words from the question, as is the case with the procedure of search engines; rather, the aim is to generate an answer that is as correct and competent as possible. As an example, consider a question from the quiz show Jeopardy: "What are the three throwing objects in the Olympic decathlon?" The correct answer is: discus, shot, and javelin. However, if you enter this question as a search in a conventional search engine, you will of course immediately get a hit based on the keyword decathlon, namely the associated Wikipedia article. This article, however, does not contain a single occurrence of the word throwing object, so that it is not directly possible to infer the three objects here. A human user would read the article and identify the objects mentioned there as throwing objects and then generate an answer. DQA is precisely about performing this task automatically. The aforementioned quiz show Jeopardy is a good test for this. In 2013, IBM's Watson system won convincingly on this show against two human contestants. Now these were not randomly selected contestants, rather they were two champions who had already won a lot of money on these shows. The remarkable thing about this is that the quiz requires an extremely broad range of knowledge areas, and the key is to answer the questions as quickly as possible. So the system must have access to very large amounts of knowledge and also process it quickly. Formalized knowledge bases – mostly in different variants of logics – are now available for a wide variety of subject areas as well as for general knowledge; however, for a powerful system like Watson, natural language texts, such as reference books, must also be used. For this purpose, the system should be able to understand the graphics and images.

How difficult it is to answer questions that involve everyday knowledge is shown by the following example, which comes from the problem collection COPA (Choice of Plausible Answers [12]). These examples require versatile knowledge that we humans use completely unconsciously, but AI systems have to search for and use specifically. Therefore, these collections are excellent for testing and evaluating AI systems. The task here is a fact, e.g. "My body casts a shadow over the grass", which is presented to a system along with a question and two alternative answers. In our example, the question is "What was the CAUSE of this?" and the alternatives are "The sun was rising." and "The grass was cut." The system must now choose the more plausible of the two answers. One easily realizes the knowledge required to answer such questions, which are trivial to humans. One must know that shadows are produced by illumination, and that the rising sun is a source of light. On the other hand, the nature of the grass has little to do with the casting of shadows. The problem for an artificial system here is to find and then process these relevant pieces of knowledge. IBM's Watson system for DQA mentioned above is now not only being used in quiz shows, rather IBM is marketing this technique as a new paradigm for software development. Cognitive computing is the term used to describe software products that can cooperate with human users to solve problems that neither humans nor machines could handle alone. In many different areas of life, the processing of vast amounts of knowledge and information in real time can thus be used to support human users. A prominent example of this is the support of doctors and scientists in cancer research; here, the immense flood of new findings and publications can be processed with the help of DQA techniques and then made available to doctors in a targeted manner.

Autonomous Vehicles

Autonomous vehicles have been researched since the 1970s. One of the pioneers is Ernst Dickmanns, who had a van equipped with computers and sensors driving on motorways as early as the 1980s. At that time, the computing power of computers was limited and the camera technology used was insufficient, but Dickmanns was nevertheless able to cover many thousands of kilometres on European roads with his research vehicles. A breakthrough came when Sebastian Thrun, then a Stanford professor, won the 2005 DARPA Grand Challenge with a Volkswagen Tuareg. The task was to complete a 132-mile circuit in the Mojave Desert within 10 h. The year before, the competition was also held, but out of more than 100 participants, not a single one was able to complete the task – the most successful vehicle only managed 7.4 miles. Just one year later, in 2005, there were four vehicles that completed the course within the time limit. Developments have continued at a similar pace, with autonomous vehicles now driving on public roads and having a major impact on the automotive industry. Techniques that enable autonomous driving are diverse and, as already mentioned above, must be interlinked. Cameras or laser rangefinders are used to generate 3D models of the vehicle's environment, learning methods are used to interpret the images and environment models and to detect and assess situations, and highly precise maps are also used where possible, for example, to record traffic lights and even the height at which they are located. In the automotive industry, a trend can be observed that aims to gradually increase autonomy through assistance systems. Attempts are being made to relieve the human driver more and more: the vehicle parks automatically, it maintains the lane and distance, it drives autonomously at low speed in traffic jams, and it brakes in the event of sudden obstacles. The driver remains in the center, the vehicle is not (yet) a robot; by this the acceptance of AI technology seems greater. It is therefore not surprising that in the field of self-driving cars, in addition to the classic and established car-makers, companies such as Tesla or even software giants such as Google or its Chinese counterpart Baidu are shaping the development and taking more radical paths.

At this point, the social significance of robotics or AI technologies in general becomes clear: Who is liable in the event of accidents that could be caused by autonomous vehicles? How should the automaton behave in situations that require ethical or moral consideration (this question is rarely asked of human drivers, by the way)? How do we behave in the context of the development of autonomous military weapons systems? We will discuss these questions in more detail in Chap. 8 on free will.

Mathematics

Automatic reasoning and automatic proof of mathematical theorems was already a dream of the enlightened mathematician in Leibniz's time. AI research has also been concerned with the automation of logic from the beginning, and indeed some nontrivial proofs have also been found by computers; e.g., the Robins algebra problem, which had been unsolved for many decades, was proven completely automatically. In addition, numerous other applications for automatic proof systems have emerged. For example, such systems are used for the verification of software and hardware; one does not just test the systems, one proves that they have certain properties. In the case of safety-critical systems such as train control systems, one proves that certain (dangerous) states cannot occur, i.e. that the system behaves correctly under all circumstances. In the development of microprocessors, the verification of hardware has become established at the latest since the famous FDIV error in the Intel Pentium processor [13]. Although the verification of hardware or software is a time-consuming and thus cost-intensive process, it is worth the effort compared to the damage to the company's image and the costs incurred, as in the case of Intel, by extensive recall actions.

Even in a discipline like mathematics, where new results can only be achieved by extremely talented, creative and highly trained scientists, automatic proof systems are slowly establishing themselves as an important tool. An example of this is the proof of Kepler's conjecture, which mathematicians have been trying to work on since Kepler made it in 1611. The problem is how to pack spheres as tightly as possible in three-dimensional space – if a fruit seller stacking oranges now comes to mind, you're pretty close to the solution. The problem is, or rather was, the formal mathematical proof. In

1998, US mathematician Thomas Hales presented a proof that was about 250 pages of manuscript and several gigabytes of program code – part of the proof is based on computer calculations. One of the most prestigious journals, the Annals of Mathematics, submitted the proof to a panel of twelve reviewers. After four years of work, the reviewers concluded that they were "99 percent sure" that the proof was correct. Hales himself has been working with several colleagues since 2003 to formally verify his proof; in the so-called Flyspeck Project, interactive automatic proof systems were used to formalize the entire proof of Kepler's conjecture, verifying it as correct. Hales, together with 21 co-authors, published a report on this in 2017 as a conclusion to Flyspeck [14].

Go

The Chinese board game Go has long been considered a great challenge for computer programs. Go is a board game in which chance plays no role. Actually, such games are well suited for computer programs, since in every game situation the set of all possible next moves is fixed, so that the program "only" has to calculate all game situations, i.e. try them out, so to speak. However, this is just pure theory when you consider that the set of possible moves and board positions is much larger than in chess – looking far enough ahead to calculate a winning move is therefore not an option. Now, in 2015, a team from the company Google DeepMind managed for the first time to defeat a world-class human player using the program AlphaGo – a true breakthrough for artificial intelligence in the field of games. Now, it is by no means the case that an entirely new method has been invented here; rather, like many other programs before it, AlphaGo uses a common search method, namely "Monte Carlo search". What is special, however, is that before Monte Carlo search was applied, a two-step learning process took place. In a first learning step, an artificial neural network was trained so that it had learned to perform expert moves. In a second stage, AlphaGo then used this learned knowledge to play against itself, learning which of the moves were profitable. This learned knowledge could then eventually be used by Monte Carlo search. For the learning phase, a special form of neural networks was used, called Deep Neural Networks. We will discuss this in detail in Chaps. 5 and 7. In another development, the AlphaZero 2017 system showed that learning expert knowledge is not necessary at all. AlphaZero is given the rules of the game as input as its only knowledge, and then plays against itself. In doing so, it learns to play so well that it was able to win against AlphaGo. Similarly, after receiving the rules of chess as input and then learning to play chess by playing against itself, AlphaZero was able to defeat one of the world's best chess programs.

2.9   Why Only Now?

With AI techniques being used in many applications and being recognized as economic and socio-political factors in large parts of society, one may have to wonder why this is happening only now, and at such a rapid pace at that. Machine learning, now also referred to as Deep Learning, is being used in most of the successful applications. Now this is by no means a new technique. We will see in the relevant chapters that learning neural networks have existed and, of course, been used for many decades. The current success can therefore not be due to the use of the techniques, rather the general conditions are decisive: Very large amounts of data are necessary to successfully train a neural network. In the case of object classification using the image database Image Net, this is currently 14 million classified images; the situation is similar with texts for learning translators for natural languages. This situation is relatively new, it has become ideal for neural networks in recent years due to the provision of increasingly large amounts of data under the buzzword Big Data. In addition, narrow but nevertheless important fields of application for learning systems have also emerged, and finally, it should also be pointed out that special, highly parallel hardware has been developed specifically for artificial neural networks.

2.10   Strong and Weak AI

We have hopefully been able to give an impression of the state of development of AI systems with various examples. How the techniques used look in detail, will be explained in the course of this book. A common classification of AI techniques should already be mentioned here, namely the distinction between strong and weak AI: Strong AI refers to methods that have the goal of modeling as well as possible how humans act. Accordingly, an AI system that understands language would also aim to be as close as possible to the human model; or conversely, it could help to develop a model for language understanding in humans. A weak AI method is understood to be a more engineering approach to producing intelligent behavior. Flying is often used as an example of this; planes fly very well without mimicking bird flight. Here it is not the method that counts, only the result. In the following chapters, it will become clear on a case-by-case basis whether this is a strong or a weak AI approach. We will revisit this point in the epilogue at the end.

At the beginning of this chapter we had quoted the first sentence from Turing's 1950 essay, "Can machines think?". We would also like to end it with the last sentence from that essay:

"We can only see a short distance ahead, but we can see plenty there that needs to be done."

References

1. Turing AM (1950) Computing machinery and intelligence. MIND: A Q Rev Pyschol Philos 59(236):433–460
2. Furbach U (2012) Turing und Künstliche Intelligenz. Informatik Spektrum 35(4):280–286
3. Turing AM (1938) Systems of logic based on ordinals. PhD thesis. Princeton University
4. Davis M (2000) The universal computer: the road from Leibniz to Turing. Norton, New York
5. Asimov I (1942) Runaround. Street & Smith, New York
6. Barthelmeß U, Furbach U (2014) Do we need Asimov's Laws? In: Liebert W-A, Neuhaus S, Paulus D, Schaffers U (Hrsg) Künstliche Menschen: Transgressionen zwischen Körper, Kultur und Technik, Bd abs/1405.0961. Königshausen & Neumann, Würzburg
7. Barthelmeß U, Furbach U (2011) IRobot- uMan. Künstliche Intelligenz und Kultur: Eine jahrtausendealte Beziehungskiste. Springer, Berlin
8. Searle JR (1980) Minds, brains, and programs. Behav Brain Sci 3:417–424
9. Block N (1978) Troubles with functionalism. Minn Stud Philos Sci 9:261–325
10. Saygin AP, Cicekli I, Akman V (2000) Turing test: 50 years later. Mind Mach 10(4):463–518
11. Furbach U (2016) Schmuddelkind ade. Das Fachgebiet 'Künstliche Intelligenz'. Forsch Lehre 16(11):474–477
12. Maslan N, Roemmele M, Gordon AS (2015) One hundred challenge problems for logical formalizations of commonsense psychology. In Twelfth International Symposium on Logical Formalizations of Commonsense Reasoning, Stanford, CA
13. Wikipedia (2018) Pentium-FDIV-Bug – Wikipedia, Die freie Enzyklopädie Stand 4. November 2018
14. Hales T, Adams M, Bauer G, Dang TD, Harrison J, Hoang LT, Kaliszyk C, Magron V, Mclaughlin S, Nguyen TT et al (2017) A formal proof of the Kepler conjecture, Bd 5. Cambridge University Press, Cambridge

3

Mind and Body

Abstract The relationship between body and mind in AI and in scientific and philosophical studies is discussed. Mostly, historical circumstances and the resulting living conditions determine people's attitudes towards this relationship. We touch upon the development of the ideas of the Baroque, the Age of Enlightenment, Classicism, Romanticism, Realism, and ultimately the philosophers of life of the twentieth century. Corresponding developments in AI can be assigned to the transformation of the respective ideologies.

In AI, the relationship between the machine and analytical performance or the digital computer (memory, arithmetic unit and control unit) and program control plays an important role. The goal of bringing machines to autonomous thinking is therefore coupled to the question of how thinking works in humans. We therefore pursue the question of the relationship between body and mind in humans.

In school, especially in physical education classes, you always get to hear the saying "mens sana in corpora sano" (a healthy mind in a healthy body). A very simple formula, which even contributed and still contributes to uphold a certain ideological principle, which more or less says, for a healthy mind you need a healthy body. But the simple attribution of mind and body is based on a fatal misinterpretation, or rather on a wrong, because abbreviated, way of quoting. The Roman satirist Juvenal (60–127 AD) mocked the Romans, who made silly requests to the gods, wishing, for example, to be rich, powerful, beautiful and successful. He thought that the gods already knew what was good for people. Nevertheless, if you want to ask for something, you should

© The Author(s), under exclusive license to Springer Fachmedien Wiesbaden GmbH, part of Springer Nature 2023

U. Barthelmeß, U. Furbach, *A Different Look at Artificial Intelligence*, https://doi.org/10.1007/978-3-658-38474-6_3

wish for mental and physical health: "Orandum est, ut sit mens sana in corpore sano" [1]. The message is clear: a healthy body does not necessarily have a healthy mind. This, however, can or should be desired. Juvenal also takes a side blow at the sports stars of his time, who were often said to lack mental abilities. We do not want to exclude that a healthy body can accommodate a healthy mind, but we reject the one-sided implicative link.

The antagonism of body and mind is not only encountered in this saying. Whenever we deal with the subject of spirit, mind or memory, its counterpart, the body, joins it in some form like a satellite. So it is not surprising that a balanced healthy relationship between body and mind is fundamentally sought in medicine. Health is an important prerequisite for survival in nature. Man is a natural being who wants to survive and reproduce in and with the help of nature. Therefore, he does well to keep his body and mind healthy. It has been found, not surprisingly, that walking in the woods is good for the body and mind.[1] Scientific studies have shown that forest air contains extremely low levels of dust particles (about 1–10% of the concentration in cities), and that oxygen, essential fragrances and tranquillity have a positive effect on physical and mental health. In the case of forest walkers, blood pressure has fallen significantly, lung capacity has increased and the elasticity of the arteries has improved. It seems that forest air is particularly good for the cardiovascular system. Scientists at the Nippon Medical School in Tokyo found that walking in the forest apparently activates cancer-killer cells, and this effect lasts for at least seven days after the walks. There is even speculation that walkers in the woods benefit from phytoncydes; these are substances that plants make to protect themselves from pathogens. The effect on the mind and spirit of both the healthy and the sick has also been researched, and the forest has been attested to clear the mind, lift mood and self-esteem, and relieve stress.

3.1   Body and Mind Over Time

Of course, the relationship between body and mind, or body and soul, has always been the subject of philosophy and theology. It was subject to strong fluctuations in the course of history. This is due to the respective spirit of the times, whose view of the world and of man is oriented towards the respective conditions of life.

---

[1] http://www.spiegel.de/gesundheit/psychologie/waldspaziergaenge-warum-sie-fuer-koerper-und-geist-gesund-sind-a-952492.html, accessed August 27, 2016.

The attitude towards the physical in the Baroque period is rather ambivalent. In this period, people were under enormous pressure: the Thirty Years' War, the accompanying catastrophes such as plague, poverty, hunger, flight focused all thoughts and feelings on the omnipresence of death. The motto of life is "memento mori" (remember that you are mortal). There are two opposite reactions to this: an extreme turning to the physical or an extreme turning away from the physical. On the one hand, one rushes to the pleasures of this world, of life, in order to take advantage of the here and now under the motto of "carpe diem". The sensual pleasures of the Baroque and the playfulness of the Rococo owe much to this appeal. On the other hand, one despairs in the face of the threat of death and resigns oneself to "vanitas" (Latin for empty appearance, nothingness, vanity): when everything must give way to time, one should regard this world as void and direct one's hopes to the hereafter. The physical experiences a strong devaluation in this attitude towards life. Since everything creaturely points to its possible decay, anything that reminds one of it is repressed – in the better circles. One thinks of Le Nôtre's gardens and parks, which seek to subdue the naturalness, the wild growth of plants through geometric arrangements and the appropriate trimming of bushes and hedges. Fashion is meant to distract from the true natural dimensions of the body and thus its mortality. Appearance conceals being, since the latter is subject to fate.

After the Thirty Years' War, the Age of Enlightenment (the term is derived from meteorology) provides more clarity. It clears up with superstition and dull surrender of man to fate. The terms Age of Enlightenment, in French Siècle des Lumières (century of lights) make it clear that it was a current of thought that sought to lead people out of the darkness of centuries of ignorance into the light of truth, so to speak. It wants to bring light into the darkness of life. It places the human being in the centre of interest and gives him self-consciousness. The mind – as an outstanding feature of man – is isolated from the body. René Descartes, philosopher, mathematician and natural scientist in the seventeen century, should be mentioned here as the founder of the so-called ontological dualism. From him comes the saying "cogito ergo sum" – I think, therefore I am. He assumes that there are two different substances: matter and spirit; everything that is decomposes into the two substances. He draws a picture of man who receives stimuli through the sense organs (material substance) and transmits them to the brain, where they then act on the immaterial mind. Kant's appeal "sapere aude" (dare to know) is addressed to man's ability to think and his willpower, who should make use of his intellect of his own free will, which distinguishes him from the animal, which is subject to corporeality. However, the enthusiasm for criticism incited by the Age of Enlightenment also called philosophers onto the scene who investigated the question, which had received little attention until then, of what was nature about man. By this they meant the "animal nature" of man, i.e. what man has in common with the animal, reproductive instinct, instinct of self-preservation, etc.

De Sade, for example, believes that man is inherently evil, that is, animalistic and libidinous, and vividly – and gleefully – illuminates the darkest corners of the heart and the repressed urges in his writings. He believes that man's nature drives him to do evil with lust. The two erotic adventure novels "La Nouvelle Justine" and "Juliette" pay homage to the instinctive human who follows the laws of blindly destructive nature and indulges in vice with pleasure without remorse. The immoral Juliette becomes rich and happy, the moral virgin Justine is struck dead by lightning – even heaven takes the side of vice! The novels are a response to the virtuous man of nature Rousseau.

Rousseau assumes that man would be good by nature if civilization did not make him what he is. In his main work "Émile, or On Education", he describes the upbringing of a boy who is largely kept away from social influences, unfolds his own nature in the open air and develops into a mature person who can move in society.

The idea of the natural human, who stands opposite the cultural human as something higher, is taken up by the poets of the "Sturm und Drang" ("Storm and Stress"). Nature becomes the epitome of the primordial, elemental, divine and is no longer the rationally ordered as in the Age of Enlightenment. The "strongman", the self-helper, was regarded as the true human being: e.g. Goethe's Götz von Berlichingen or Schiller's Karl Moor – "O pfui über dieses schlappe Kastratenjahrhundert!"[2] [2], in whom thought and action form a unity, who is master of his spiritual, mental, and physical powers, who remains true to himself and is not afraid to take on a whole world – even at the price of ruin.

This radicalism gives way to the moderate concept of classicism, which strives for harmony between body, mind and emotion. Already in his dissertation of the medical faculty on the "Ueber den Zusammenhang der thierischen Natur des Menschen mit seiner geistigen." Schiller explains that a person who suffers mentally can become physically ill, and whoever is physically ill can recover through positive mental experiences. The physical condition influences the mental and vice versa. He concludes, "... der Mensch ist nicht Seele und Körper, der Mensch ist die innigste Vermischung dieser beiden Substanzen"[3] [3].

---

[2] O fie on this limp castrato century!

[3] ... man is not soul and body, man is the most intimate blending of these two substances

Schiller also literally experienced the dialectical interplay of mind and body in his own body and expressed it in his work. Schiller, who was plagued by many illnesses (malaria, pneumonia, the symptoms of which had only worsened as a result of mistreatment), fought throughout his short life – he only lived to be 46 – against the deterioration of his body with the help of his mental strength through disciplined creative work. The doctor who performed his autopsy after his death wrote in his findings that one must wonder how the poor man could have lived so long under these circumstances [4]. Schiller also opposed the state body, the political circumstances under which Schiller had to live, the constriction of his personal development by the despot Karl Eugen von Württemberg (drill in the Karlsschule, total surveillance, spying, etc.) with his devotedly championed utopia of a free nation-state. He seeks to overcome the intolerability of physical as well as political conditions with the ideal of a liberal attitude and form of government. He has the Marquis Posa in "Don Carlos" say, "Sire, give freedom of thought!" The world of the mind gives him scope to create a better, ideal world. In Wallenstein it is said, that it is the mind that builds the body [4]. The term "Spielraum" (playground) refers to the method Schiller and also his kindred spirit Goethe use to achieve their goals. The playground is aesthetics, the artistic fiction that enables man to experience himself as a holistic ideal being outside of his everyday life that alienates him, free of existential constraints.

The background to this strategy is political. The Weimar classics feared that the excesses of the French Revolution might spread to Germany. The mass executions witnessed by the onlooking people served to satisfy their desire for revenge. The revolution, which was supposed to create justice, perverted into arbitrary acts of violence that satisfied the desire for power of individuals. Insecurity, fear and horror – la terreur – took over. The movement triggered by reason was infiltrated and disintegrated by instinct-driven impulses: "The revolution eats its own children!" Therefore, the classics wanted to educate people to be humane beings who would make proper use of their physical as well as mental powers, and not fall prey to plebeian impulses. The right dose of reason and feeling should prevent them from obeying their instincts and lead them to act prudently. We will discuss this aspect in more detail later when we examine "free will" (see Chap. 8).

The Romanticism perceives the classical principle of balancing emotion and reason as a constricting corset. Romanticism sees itself as a counter-draft to the "pure reason" of the Age of Enlightenment, the ideal of the Classicism period and the emerging industrial age. It focuses on the world of feelings, moods and sensations, the primordial, the miraculous and the mystical. Nature in its originality and infinity, animate in its eyes, is a symbol of human sensations. It sees in the classical concept a shortening of human dispositions, even a castration of human potentials. Where is there room for the fantastic, the mysterious, the inexplicable? Why should areas of life be excluded that move one but cannot be explained? Hence the Romanticism postulate the primacy of the immeasurable, the intangible, the fantastic, the unconscious, the mysterious, the irrational. They want one thing above all, to get away from what they see as the stuffy philistines who settle into the comfortable bourgeoisie of their superficial world. Their flight from reality is also due to the desolate political situation. The Restoration, which began with the Congress of Vienna, dashed hopes of the formation of a German nation-state with a liberal constitution. The progressing industrialization degraded the people more and more to their economic benefit. The self-realization of the individual in society, aspired to by the classicists, has proved – in the eyes of the romanticists – to be an illusion. So all that remains is the flight inwards and the longing for a dream world. The average, the finite, the ordinary – reality – acquires a higher, mysterious meaning and the appearance of infinity through the remedy of romanticization. At the expense of reality, the materially and physically experienceable world, the fleeting and elusive soul and the fantasizing, playful spirit have a boom.

In time, however, the romantic spell had to give way to the pressures of political reality and the frustration of oppressed citizens: The princes had lured their peoples into the war against Napoleon with the promise of a constitution that guaranteed civil liberties and citizen participation in government. Instead, pre-revolutionary conditions were restored, restorative measures whipped through. It is becoming increasingly clear to people how dependent they are on the circumstances of their lives. Their existence is determined by the reality of their surroundings, their biological and sociological premises. The character and destiny of human beings are determined by the historical time in which they live, the psychological heredity as well as the milieu (cf. Karl Marx, Auguste Comte, Hippolyte Taine and Charles Darwin). Thus, an about-face to Romanticism takes place. The positivism of the realists places the material, the empirically measurable and determined by reason and logic, in the foreground. The various realist currents (more or less political, more or less literary, more or less scientific) lead to correspondingly different and sometimes radical expressions of materialism. The aspect of the physical has the upper hand here.

The one-sided reduction of man to what can be grasped by the natural sciences and the determinism based on this is countered by the philosophers of life, developed in France by Henri Bergson and in Germany by Wilhelm Dilthey. Man is to be seen in his wholeness; the concrete experience of man, shaped by social and historical conditions, by reason as well as by intuition, instinct, drives and will, is at the centre of their way of thinking. The philosopher and phenomenologist Merleau-Ponty puts a third way to the side of the either-or of body and mind by trying to fully overcome the Cartesian division of substance into body and mind (res extensa and res cogitans) through his body phenomenology (Chap. 11).

We would like to state here that both factors, body and mind, are in a relationship of tension, that they have taken on a different significance in the course of history, and that they are linked to one another by nature, the moment of the natural or the creative.

3.2   AI: Intelligence Without a Body?

Back to Descartes: He understands the human being as a kind of mechanical automaton that also has a soul that is separate from and independent of the body (i.e. autonomous). A similar view could be attributed to the early beginners in AI research. The body as such plays only a subordinate role: cogito ergo sum.

Take a sophisticated and efficient machine as a brain, equip it with a few sensors and try to solve an "intellectual task". Examples include playing chess, understanding natural language texts, analysing images or solving mathematical problems. The first robots were also constructed according to this principle – a computer on wheels that had at most a few sensors. One of the first mobile systems was developed at Stanford's AI lab and is now considered the system that helped lay the first foundations for modern autonomous robotic systems. The system was called Shakey – it was a man-sized structure with electronics on wheels, connected by a cable to the actual computer in the next room. Shakey's electronics consisted of sensors and actuators, the actual computer was still too big to be on board at the time. The name came from the peculiarity that the robot had to take long pauses (where the computer was working) between each action it performed, resulting in shaky movements of the robot. Again, the principle behind this form of robotics research was to program a powerful computer so that the mobile computer was able to solve tasks on its own. These were mostly simple planning tasks in a simplified world consisting of blocks of different shapes and colors. The robot was then supposed to find a particular block and move it in a predetermined way. A major success of this early robotics research was the development and use of special programming languages with which such tasks could be solved.

So the performance of the robot was essentially determined by the performance of the computer, the brain – cogito ergo sum.

Throughout AI research, Descartesian dualism has taken the form of the so-called symbol-processing hypothesis. This states that any form of intelligent behavior or action is to be achieved by a symbol-processing system.

This hypothesis is adopted by many AI researchers as a working basis. It means that the approach of currently available computers is suitable for programming intelligent or cognitive systems. On the one hand, the roots of this view go back to the Age of Enlightenment, as discussed above, but on the other hand they touch on the whole foundation of theoretical computer science. In the 1920s, philosophers and mathematicians had already asked themselves what it meant for something to be computable. So, long before computers were available in their present form, there was discussion about whether there were functions (in the mathematical sense) that could not be computed. Independently of each other, various imaginary machines were developed to define the term "computable".

Common is the abstract model of a machine by Alan Turing, the Turing machine named after him. It has a tape on which characters can be written and erased again. The tape has unlimited length and can be seen as an ideal, arbitrarily available memory. Above the tape there is a read/write head, which can read the character on the field below and also print a new character on the tape. Furthermore this head can move the tape to the left or to the right by one field at a time. This is already the whole (imaginary) hardware of the Turing machine. It also has software, a program that controls the actions of the read/write head. It consists of a sequence of instructions, such as "when the character 1 is read, replace it with a space and move the head one space to the right". Now write a given problem on the tape, for example 111 + 11111, so "add 3 and 5" and start the program with the instructions to the read/write head. When the machine finally stops and there is the string 11111111 on the tape, you say the machine has calculated this as the result of the input. As simple as this machine model seems, it is so powerful that it can be used to describe the operation of computers commonly used today. All other alternative machine models that have been developed so far can also be traced back to the Turing machine. There is therefore reason to believe that this type of symbol processing is powerful enough to solve cognitive and intelligent tasks. Turing himself raised the question of whether machines can think back in the 1950s [5]. We will discuss this in more detail in Chap. 11 on consciousness.

In many areas of AI research, this reliance on the symbol-processing hypothesis has led to spectacular successes, and of course there are other interesting and challenging tasks in these subfields of AI. Nonetheless, since the late 1980s, a view has been established that was then labeled "Nouvelle AI". Rodney Brooks was one of the pioneers of this new kind of AI, which he describes very catchily in his paper "Elephants don't play Chess" [6].

Instead of relying exclusively on the symbol-processing hypothesis to develop intelligent systems, he proposes anchoring systems in the physical world by means of sensors and actuators. Only in this way, he argues, is it possible to generate intelligence. Brooks cites evolution as an example – he argues that artificial systems should first be taught to move, react and all that is necessary for survival. Only then, he says, can reasoning, problem solving, language and expert knowledge be tackled. In a sense, this means giving greater space to physicality in the development of intelligent systems. Brooks develops beetle-like robots that have a very simple computer core, and he shows that these robots can use it to learn to coordinate their legs and use them to move around. Brooks thus establishes a line of research in AI and robotics that views the body and mind as a single entity in which no part can be developed in isolation from each other.

All this is actually not at all surprising, if one considers the many results from psychology and neuroscience on the body-mind problem. Two phenomena should be mentioned here: firstly, the effect of phantom pain. People who have had a part of their body amputated can often clearly feel pain in the part that is no longer there. The brain presumably simulates the painful limb through a form of memory. Second, there is an experiment, first described in [7], that anyone can easily perform for themselves: Sit down at a table, place both hands on the table-top, one hand, let us suppose the left, being so concealed by a box or the like that one cannot see it oneself. Instead of the covered left hand, place a rubber glove on the top so that it is placed next to the right hand in a place where the left might normally lie. A helper now strokes the covered left hand and the rubber hand, in complete synchrony. After some time, the rubber hand "feels" like part of one's own body. The brain has, so to speak, expanded the body. There are different variants of this experiment, in which one can even do without the trick of concealing a hand and the test person can even feel the third artificial hand as his own.

The connection between body and mind is also a central theme in the millennia-old tradition of various yoga schools and directions. Already in the underlying writings of yoga, the Yogasutra of the philosopher Patañjali (pre-sumably lived between the second and third century AD), all possible aspects of physicality, mind and consciousness are dealt with. Thus, Patañjali presents the path of yoga as an eight-linked construction kit, in which the mastery of the body through exercises (asanas), the control of breathing (pranayama), the mastery of the senses and concentration play an important role. Only then can meditation and a special state of consciousness called samadhi be achieved. A detailed treatment of the development of yoga can be found in [8], where it is also very well understood that to the spread of modern yoga in the West since the nineteenth century, the emphasis on the body and not only the philosophical tradition has played an important role.

3.3 AI and Transhumanism

We have long been accustomed to augmenting our mental abilities. Whether it's the abacus to improve our computing power or Wikipedia as a ubiquitous source of knowledge, humans are accustomed to using new technologies to enhance or augment them. Of course, the same is true for the body: the 2016 annual report of the German Society for Orthopaedics and Orthopaedic Surgery lists 137,000 implantations of artificial hip joints. Implants of pace-makers and artificial hearts have become just as common. These are only a few examples; in the field of prosthesis development and especially in the control of prostheses, there are developments that actually represent an inter-play of artificial body (part) and mind. In myoelectric arm prostheses, nerve signals are generated by muscle contractions, which are then used by the prosthesis as control signals. However, direct control by brain activity is also possible; here, activations of brain structures are used directly to control the prosthesis.

So we can say with a clear conscience that extensions, additions or renewals of humans by technical systems are quite a reality. In science fiction literature, people are described as cyborgs whose bodies have been augmented by artifi-cial components. Our examples show that this has long since become com-monplace. Now we can further assess this development, and in doing so we can of course also take into account the rapid further development in areas of artificial intelligence.

Assuming the development of technology to date, using what is known as Moore's Law as a basis for calculation, it is possible to predict the approach of a singularity. Moore's Law is based on a prediction made by Gordon Moore in

1965, where he states that the number of transistors that can be placed in an integrated circuit is doubling every year. This exponential growth in computer technology has proven true over the past few decades, so it does not seem unrealistic to assume the same growth in the future. The Singularity refers to a turning point at which the interaction between humans and artificial intelligence has become so advanced that a superintelligence is emerging that is self-evolving and can no longer be controlled by us humans. A prominent representative of this thesis is Ray Kurzweil. In his bestseller [9], the renowned computer scientist, inventor and entrepreneur Kurzweil analyses the development of AI research and predicts that by 2029 it will be possible to emulate the entire human brain in a digital computer. Such systems could then be analysed and developed so that by 2045 they will have radically modified and evolved themselves so that the Singularity can take place. This superintelligence can then spread from our planet until it takes over the entire universe. This sounds like modern science fiction, but it certainly has roots in philosophy and even theology. The very aspect of humanity becoming one with the universe is startlingly reminiscent of the teachings of Pierre Teilhard de Chardin. This Jesuit, theologian and natural scientist had already written about the further development of man at the beginning of the twentieth century. His writings were rejected by the Vatican, and it was only after his death in 1955 that they were published and received much attention. In his pivotal book, "Der Mensch im Kosmos" [10] de Chardin describes humanity and the universe as evolving and moving toward an end point, the "Point Omega," where man, the universe, and God become one. This view is also taken up by contemporary cosmologists.

Possibly the term transhumanism also comes to mind on this topic. The direction of singularitarianism just described can certainly be understood as a form of transhumanism. In other forms of transhumanism the transcendence to a superintelligence is not so much in the foreground, rather mankind is supposed to develop further, possibly also with the help of modern technologies. Transhumanism aims at a significant extension of the lifespan, increase of intelligence and the general well-being of humans through technological aids. For the direction of transhumanism, which is influenced by the teachings of Teilhard de Chardin, the term "Christian transhumanism" is also used.

It is remarkable that the fusion of humans and technology in transhumanism can even be tolerated from a Christian point of view. In contrast, one finds much more often reluctance or skepticism towards robots. In [11] we argued that the creation of robots can be understood in our Western, Christian culture as an attempt to create life. This means, in the final analysis, that humans presume to do godlike things. Such attempts are described many times, e.g. the Tower of Babel or the creation of the Golem in Prague, and always lead to a punishment of the presuming human. In the case of transhumanism, however, it is not new and living things that are created by humans, but rather humans are developed further and perfected. This can certainly be understood in the sense of the Christian doctrine of creation.

3.4 Summary

Starting from the antagonism of body and mind, we have discussed how the relationship between body and mind has changed in cultural history. From the Baroque to the Age of Enlightenment, body and mind were radically separated; the mind is the outstanding feature of the human being and is isolated from the body. It is only in the Classical period that the harmony of mind, body and feeling is again sought, which we have shown with the example of the Weimar Classics.

A similar development can be observed in the (comparatively short) history of AI. In the early days of AI, people tended to focus on computers that were as smart as possible; the symbol processing hypothesis dominated research. A robot was a computer that was mobile, a brain on wheels, so to speak. Analogous to the classical era, the relationship between body and mind has fundamentally changed here due to the "Nouvelle AI" approach. The body and being embedded in the environment is considered a basic prerequisite for intelligent behaviour – just as evolution has taught us. If one follows the transhumanists, evolution continues to the singularity, where body, mind and AI become one.

References

1. Juvenalis. Decimes iunius. (1993) Satiren, X 356. Artemis & Winkler, München
2. Schiller F (2005) Die Räuber. Deutscher Taschenbuch Verlag, München
3. Schiller F (1879) Ueber den Zusammenhang der thierischen Natur des Menschen mit seiner geistigen. Schillers Sämmtliche Werke, Bd 4. J. G. Cotta'sche Buchhandlung, Stuttgart
4. Soboczynski A (2009) Friedrich Schiller. Die Zeit, 12. Dezember, Nr 47
5. Turing AM (1950) Computing machinery and intelligence. MIND: Q Rev Pyschol Philos 59(236/October):433–460

6. Brooks RA (1990) Elephants don't play chess. Robot Auton Syst 6:3–15

7. Lenggenhager B, Tadi T, Metzinger T, Blanke O (2007) Video ergo sum: manipulating bodily self-consciousness. Science 317(5841):1096–1099

8. Singleton M (2010) Yoga body. The origins of modern posture practice. Oxford University Press, Oxford

9. Kurzweil R (2005) The singularity is near: when humans transcend biology. Penguin, London

10. De Chardin PT (2005) Der Mensch im Kosmos, Bd 1055. Beck, München

11. Barthelmeß U, Furbach U (2014) Do we need Asimov's laws? In: Liebert WA, Neuhaus S, Paulus D, Schaffers U (Hrsg) Künstliche Menschen: Transgressionen zwischen Körper, Kultur und Technik, Bd abs/1405.0961. Königshausen & Neumann, Würzburg

4

Time and Memory

Abstract When it comes to the representation of temporal processes, a differentiated approach to time is required in AI. Time and memory play a central role in our lives. How do we manage to behave adequately? When we remember, we refer back to the past and visualize it. We do a lot without thinking, and yet we need to be awake, responsive, and creative or forward-looking. So time plays a key role in the process of remembering.

I'm always amazed when I see students who are just about to take their school leaving examination. That's unbelievable, I only had this boy in the fifth grade, he's just started and he's already supposed to be taking his school-leaving exams! I often can't believe it. In contrast, I remember very well how miserably long my own school days lasted, the years dragged on, the weeks, the hours. When will I finally be allowed to go out alone in the evening, get my driver's license? The end, the school leaving examination, seemed unattainable. But the summer holidays also lasted much longer, I spent countless, endless days in the open-air swimming pool, the winters offered extended afternoons on which I could go sledging or ice-skating.

I am not alone in feeling the altered perception of time. Ionesco explains it in terms of habit: "Habit polishes time; one glides over it as over a parquet floor waxed too smooth." [1]. He suggests as an antidote to travel a lot, "two days of travel ... outweigh thirty in the usual place ... "[1]. I can certainly agree with this, because when I travel, the days seem longer again, the unknown and the new stand up to the ingrained and the old familiar. But it is to be feared that even permanent travel will eventually succumb to the wear

© The Author(s), under exclusive license to Springer Fachmedien Wiesbaden GmbH, part of Springer Nature 2023

U. Barthelmeß, U. Furbach, *A Different Look at Artificial Intelligence*,
https://doi.org/10.1007/978-3-658-38474-6_4

and tear of habit. Habit sets in when we repeat or practice something in order to better master sequences of movements or behaviors and thus simplify our lives. It cannot be switched off and is ultimately the cornerstone of our ability to learn, store and retrieve knowledge.

Time therefore plays an important role in remembering and memory. For knowledge, learning, remembering and also forgetting are subject to the factor of time, which, as we have seen above, can be perceived quite differently. But how is time to be grasped or understood?

Since Aristotle, the idea has prevailed that time is merely a measurable movement that, coming from the past, grasps the present and flows towards the future, passing independently of a person's life. The French philosopher Henri Bergson takes a radically different view. Since we will have to deal with Bergson more often, we want to introduce him briefly here:

Henri Bergson, born in Paris in 1859

and died there in 1941, is the son of Jewish parents, his father Polish, his mother English. He grew up bilingual (French and English) and achieved brilliant academic results, which enabled him to enter the ENS, the Ecole normale supérieure, France's elite school. There he studies philosophy in the same year as the socialist leaders Jean Jaurès and Emile Durkheim, who establishes the independence of sociology as a discipline and because of his rationalist stance becomes the antagonist of the anti-rationalist philosopher Bergson. After his studies he married a cousin of the symbolist novelist Marcel Proust, whose novel cycle "Auf der Suche nach der verlorenen Zeit" would bear traces of intellectual kinship with Bergson. The latter, like other French intellectuals, first became a high school teacher and wrote minor philosophical writings and his first book, Essais sur les données immédiates de la conscience (1889), (Time and Free Will: . An essay on the immediate facts of consciousness, 1910). In 1896 he published his second major paper, "Matière et mémoire. Essais sur la relation du corps à l'esprit" (Matter and Memory 1912), in which he also takes into account the latest brain research. He was subsequently entrusted with lectures at the École Normale Supérieure in 1897 and later received a chair in modern philosophy, which he held until 1922. In his 1901 essay "Le Rire" (Laughter 1911), Bergson developed a theory of the comic and addressed the question of how the living can be described: "Le comique: du mécanique plaqué sur du vivant ..." (The comic: the mechanical superimposed onto the living)". At the same time, he developed a theory of artistic creativity that made him a prophet of symbolist artists and writers. He also attracted attention abroad. At the First International Congress of Philosophers in Paris in August 1900, he delivered the lecture "Sur les origines psychologiques de notre croyance à la loi de causalité" (Psychological origins of our belief in the law of causality), which expressed Bergson's non-rationalist tendency. The third major work, L'Évolution créatrice (Creative Evolution, 1911), published in 1907, is a contribution to the theory of evolution, whose determinism Bergson criticized. This work is indexed by the Church.

(continued)

(continued)

In 1911, at the International Congress of Philosophers in Bologna, Bergson delivers the lecture "L'Intuition philosophique" (Philosophical Intuition), which addresses the importance of intuition – understood as a precise philosophical method – in his thought. Bergson was awarded numerous honours and distinctions and was entrusted with diplomatic duties during the First World War. Like Albert Einstein, with whom he discussed the concept and nature of time in detail, he was a member of the League of Nations Commission, the predecessor institution of UNESCO. In 1927 he was awarded the Nobel Prize for Literature, mainly for his works "Le rire" and "L'évolution créatrice". In his late work "Les deux sources de la morale et de la religion" (1932) (The Two Sources of Morality and Religion, 1935), he approaches Christian ideas, but does not convert, as he does not want to betray his Jewish fellow citizens, who are increasingly exposed to reprisals. Thus, over 80 years old, he renounces his awards, titles and related privileges. In 1940, while waiting for hours in a queue to register as a Jew, he contracted a severe case of pneumonia from which he would not recover. A year later he dies.

Back to Bergson's concept of time, which is an important building block of his philosophy. Although he recognizes the physical space-time, "le temps" (time), which can be measured quantitatively with clocks, he opposes it with another form of time, which cannot be divided into units such as seconds or minutes and is perceived qualitatively as individually experienced or lived time, which he calls "la durée" (duration) [2]. In everyday language, when we speak of felt time or felt age, we may come a little closer to the concept of "durée". Subjective time is to be understood as duration, not as a collection of discrete points, separate, measurable moments. It is about a continuum of contents of a personal nature that have occurred spontaneously, are irreversible, and shape the biography of the individual, rather than contents that have been learned through repetition, forming fixed patterns of habits and automatisms that we apply without remembering the situations of learning. When we recite a poem by heart, we do not, Bergson says, usually have the history of memorization and repetition before our eyes. It is – like all habit-based activities in our lives – reflexively present.

Duration, on the other hand, is comparable to the tree that grows and changes, preserves itself and changes at the same time. It constitutes the individual, changes according to the added experiences, which in turn are oriented to the existing memory images, and forms something new, creative. Contrary to what the term might suggest – duration might be thought of as something permanent, constant – it is subject to constant change and continues to develop. This duration is the basis of intuition, an approach to gaining insight that seeks to grasp the human being holistically, namely as a mind being and a living being acting in nature. We will return to intuition in Chap. 9 on creativity.

The two temporal components "durée" and "temps" correspond to the "moi intérieur", the real self, and the "moi conventionnel", the conventional, superficial self, which is adapted to momentary circumstances. In the real self, based on duration, the "élan vital" (vital impetus) comes to fruition, which gives man the freedom to develop and complete himself. Finding the past again as duration is the core theme of Proust's novel cycle "Auf der Suche nach der verlorenen Zeit" [3].

4.1   Time in Artificial Systems

Of course, the representation of time also plays an important role in AI research. On the one hand, it can be used to determine the sequence of events or actions, but on the other hand, it can also be used to make the truth content of statements time-dependent. Suppose that in a logic-based knowledge base, the level of a car tank is represented by the phrase *tank _ level(full)*, then this is always the case – it cannot simultaneously be true that the tank is not full: ¬*tank _ level(full)* (¬ is to be read here as "not"). In other words, we cannot change the level of the tank without violating the rules of classical logic. Now, taking time to be a discrete sequence of instants 1, 2, 3, ⋯, we can give the expression *tank _ level* an instant as an additional argument. We can then use this to formulate *tank _ level(full*, 1) and simultaneously ¬*tank _ level(full*, 7). At time 1, the tank would thus be full and at time 7 it would not be full, which may well make sense if the tank had been emptied between 1 and 7. Now this procedure can be criticized with the argument that time is not discrete but continuously progressing. We could not insert a point in time between two directly successive points in time if we proceeded discretely. Indeed, in physics, time is also represented by a real number. Usually then, functions that are time-dependent are also continuous functions, so the usual mathematical tool repertoire can be used to describe these functions. This conception and representation of time would correspond to Bergson's "temps"; but "durée" can also be found in the AI context.

Here there is the alternative of dispensing with a direct representation of time and instead using events to indicate points in time. For example, this is how one usually proceeds when writing cooking recipes: "Heat the onions in the pan until they are translucent, then add the rice while stirring." Here it is completely irrelevant how long the onions take, the important event is that they become translucent. "Finally, the rice is cooked, adding liquid constantly, until it is soft and creamy." More time than was necessary to cook the onions certainly passes before this event occurs. We are not interested, however, in the absolute periods of time; what is interesting is merely the occurrence of the event, and the fact that they can be put in order. With this approach, it is also easy – unlike the discrete case from above – to slip a new event between two successive ones: "While the rice is cooking, cut the vegetables ...". Instead of making time points explicit, events are used to name time points or intervals and to relate them to each other.

Another possibility would be to dispense with a reference to time altogether and instead represent only different states: If we take an assembly robot as an example, we are interested in the sequence of states the part to be assembled is in. For example, we have a car body without an engine and without wheels, a car body with an engine and without wheels, and finally a finished vehicle. The vehicle goes through a series of states, which of course were brought about in time, but without time being explicitly mentioned.

4.2   Bergson's Concept of Remembering

Bergson's concept of "durée" thus most closely resembles the approach in AI of characterizing time through individual events. His reflections on memory are based on the special importance of temporality in human life. Years before the publication of the work "Matter and Memory" [4], Nietzsche stated in his treatise "On the Usefulness and Disadvantage of History for Life" [5] that knowledge of temporality is fundamental for the formation of our memory. The memory of man is only developed in such a differentiated way because he is a historical and therefore temporal being. Animals live only in the moment and are thus apparently happy, since they know neither the burden of the past nor the worries of the future: "Betrachte die Herde, die an dir vorüberweidet: sie weiß nicht, was Gestern, was Heute ist, springt umher, frißt, ruht, verdaut, springt wieder, und so vom Morgen bis zur Nacht und von Tage zu Tage, kurz angebunden mit ihrer Lust und Unlust, nämlich an den Pflock des Augenblickes und deshalb weder schwermütig noch überdrüssig. Dies zu sehen geht dem Menschen hart ein, weil er seines Men schentums sich vor dem Tiere brüstet und doch nach seinem Glücke eifersüchtig hinblickt – denn das will er allein, gleich dem Tiere weder überdrüssig noch unter Schmerzen leben, und will es doch vergebens, weil er es nicht will wie das Tier."[1] [5].

---

[1] Consider the herd that grazes past you: it do not know what was yesterday, what is today, leaps about, eats, rests, digests, leaps again, and so from morning to night and from day to day, fettered to the moment and its pleasure and displeasure and therefore neither melancholy nor weary. It is hard for man to see this, because he boasts of his humanity before the animal and yet looks jealously at its happiness – this is what he wants, like the animal, neither to be weary nor to live in pain, and yet wants it in vain, because he does not want to be like an animal.

For Bergson, the moment of temporality is crucial for distinguishing between two types of memory: mechanical or habitual memory (analogous to the conventional self) and pure memory (analogous to the real self). The mechanical memory comprises the learned habits and automatisms that are present without the need for much thought.

Pure memory stores the individual biographical past, regardless of whether the contents are always accessible. This means, then, that what is not consciously perceived, unconscious contents, also count. This is an idea that Freud will take up later, even if his ideas differ from those of Bergson.

Now how does the interaction of soul and body or mind and body work? In his studies on "Materie und Gedächtnis" Bergson concludes that the body, always directed to activity, has the essential function of limiting the life of the spirit for the purpose of activity [4]. How is this to be understood? The body ensures that it can survive biologically and is therefore supplied with everything it needs to live. It uses perception to filter the elements of the outside world that are suitable or important for its survival. In this way he contacts only those parts of the world which his organic constitution enables him to perceive and which help him to prepare his movements. It is not, then, according to Bergson, the task of the body to store up the memories of the mind, but to select the memory useful for the present action and to make it conscious by its efficiency. An already remembered perception, which is in harmony with the present perception, is thereby called up and modifies the perception of the present sensory stimulus. In perception, therefore, two actions intertwine: the selection of a present sensory stimulus directed toward a future action and the simultaneous processing of the same from the standpoint of the past remembered.

Memories do not always have to come into play (see habitual memory). The criterion of their selection is their optimal suitability to complete and clarify the momentary situation. Memory images that are rejected because they do not seem useful or even dangerous are rejected into the realm of the unconscious or – in the psychic sense – repressed. But memories that are similar to perception enter into the movements that correspond to perception [4].

To illustrate this, let us once again draw on Bergson's comparison of memory with a tree: memory is rooted in the depths of the past. The act of remembering is both present and past. The original impression remains in latency and is retrievable until the moment when it is updated by the activity of memory.

Bergson's concept is also consistent with the current division of memory into procedural and declarative knowledge. We want to track down these two forms of memory during a run or walk in the woods. Then let's get started:

First we just walk or run, we can do that without thinking too much. How does that happen?

When we started learning to walk as toddlers, it was not so natural. As we watch them take their first steps, we realize that this form of movement is anything but familiar to us and must be painstakingly learned. The baby will try, provided it has learned to sit up after crawling, to get its sense of balance under control. It will still want to hold on to furniture and claim the helping arms of the parents. Its sensory experiences – probably including the pain of falling down – are stored first in sensory memory (ultra-short-term memory) and then in short-term memory (working memory) for only a few seconds. With appropriate repetition and practice of the movement, it is eventually stored in long-term memory. Since it is supposed to be available for recall all the time, it takes a shortcut, which means it doesn't even have to be done consciously, but is present unconsciously. The memory that stores these unconscious simple, mostly motor movements is called procedural (from Latin: procedere going forward) or implicit (from Latin implicatus: entangled, with stated, not explicit).

When we ride a bike or drive a car, dance, tie shoelaces, play the piano, we can fall back on what we have learned, which of course works better the more we have trained. The memory for these actions is located in the subcortical regions and usually functions even when memory disorders are present.

So we run without being conscious of running, so we have our head free. In the forest or in a park, there are also few disturbing factors that could interfere with this liberated movement, independent of conscious thought. Perhaps there are a few roots or stumbling blocks that we keep in mind. Otherwise, we can indulge in the benefits of walking and the forest. In his study [6] on the intelligence of plants, plant scientist Stefano Mancuso notes that we relieve stress and promote concentration more easily in their presence. He sees the reasons for this in our past and the instinctive knowledge that our species is not viable without plants [6]. Our bond with the forest probably belongs to our archaic experiences, which is also revealed by the oldest literary forms, the fairy tales.

While running, it can happen that – uncalled – thoughts and ideas arise that have perhaps only been waiting to be put to use under relaxed conditions: an old unsolved problem, a solution path, a new combination of mental connections. They may have become detached from their original holders in free space and are looking for a way to reconnect. This could be chalked up to "free association", a kind of preparation for creative work.

These awakened thoughts originate from the declarative (Latin: declarare, to proclaim, explain) or explicit (Latin: explicitus, explicit) memory. On the one hand, it stores episodes, events and facts from one's own life in the episodic memory (Greek: epeisódion, that which is still to come) and knowledge independent of one's own life, the so-called world knowledge of a person, for example professional knowledge, facts from history, politics, cooking recipes etc. in the semantic memory (from Greek: semainein: to designate). The entire neocortex is involved in declarative memory, the right frontal and temporal cortex in particular in episodic memory, and the temporal lobe in particular in semantic memory. We will discuss memory and remembering in humans in more detail in Chap. 9.

4.3 Summary

Starting from Bergson's notion of time, we have discussed different notions of time. We have seen that a similar distinction is used in AI systems. Time can be represented and implemented as a sequence of points in time or as a sequence of events or states. That time also plays a central role for remembering, we have also seen in Bergson's work. There, the connection between body and mind in remembering was also addressed.

References

1. Ionesco E (1968) Tagebuch. Journal en miettes. Luchterhand, Frankfurt a. M
2. Bergson H (2006) Zeit und Freiheit. Eine Abhandlung über die unmittelbaren Bewusstseinstatsachen. Verlag Felix Meiner, Hamburg
3. Proust M (1950) Auf der Suche nach der verlorenen Zeit. Suhrkamp, Frankfurt
4. Bergson H (2001) Materie und Gedächtnis. Eine Abhandlung über die Beziehung zwischen Körper und Geist. Verlag Felix Meiner, Hamburg
5. Nietzsche F (1951) Vom Nutzen und Nachteil der Historie für das Leben. Reclam, Stuttgart
6. Mancuso S (2015) Die Intelligenz der Pflanzen. Kunstmann, München

5

Representation of Knowledge

Abstract Knowledge representation is a task that has existed since language was written down. Various stages of scientific development lead to the fact that statements can be converted into numbers or formulas that can be read by machines. This allows artificial systems to be used to accomplish complex tasks. In AI, various techniques are used to process knowledge in the machine and to enable understanding and cooperation between machine and human.

So far we have talked exclusively about memory and remembering in humans. If we now transfer these two terms to artificial systems, we speak of knowledge representation and processing. In this chapter, we want to outline the treatment of knowledge in artificial systems, that is, in AI. A major difference from what has been covered so far in this book is that, for the first time, we will pay much greater attention to memory, i.e., the representation of knowledge. So far, we have given greater weight to remembering and not so much to the mental way of storing knowledge.

If one thinks about the possibilities of representing knowledge, the writing down of facts naturally comes to mind immediately. Nowadays, we are used to obtaining knowledge from written sources, e.g. in the form of textbooks or scientific scripts. However, the use of texts that are written in natural language is in principle only possible for humans and therefore only conditionally suitable for artificial systems – we will come back to this later and put this into perspective.

© The Author(s), under exclusive license to Springer Fachmedien Wiesbaden GmbH, part of Springer Nature 2023

U. Barthelmeß, U. Furbach, *A Different Look at Artificial Intelligence*, https://doi.org/10.1007/978-3-658-38474-6_5

However, this seemingly obvious method of using texts as a representation of knowledge is by no means self-evident. If we go back to ancient Greece, we find written records there that were written more for the purpose of being read aloud. In scrolls, text was written down in strings without spaces or punctuation, sometimes even changing the direction of writing at the end of the line "furrow-like". This so-called "scriptura continua" can still be found today in various Asian writing systems. The texts of ancient Greece could only be read aloud in this form, and only then did they acquire structure and arrangement. In poetry, the verse metre, which played an important role in reading aloud, also helped to structure the text. Texts often recorded speeches so that they could be repeated at any time by reading them aloud – the written form was, so to speak, a continuation of oral speech. Scientific discourse took place through speech and counter-speech. The transition from linguistic discourse to discourse with the aid of texts, i.e. to prose discourse, took place only slowly. Only by separating the text from the spoken language did it become expedient to structure the text, making it easier to read and understand. Our use of punctuation marks, headings, and page breaks did not become clearly established until much later in scholasticism, that is, in the High Middle Ages.

However, an exception to this scriptura continua can already be found in ancient Greece, namely in the use of ideographic signs in algebra and geometry. Ideographic signs are stylized images that stand for a concept or, rather, the idea of a concept. For example, the superscript 2 in the algebraic term x^2 stands for the concept of squaring a number x. It is also clear here that the two-dimensionality of the medium of paper or papyrus is exploited. Many centuries before Christ, it was clear to Greek mathematicians and philosophers that in order to convey mathematical facts, ideas and concepts had to be written down, which in turn would then be comprehended by the reader. The representation of knowledge in written form played an important role in ancient Greece; the term "techne", from which our word technique is derived, denotes a form of practical knowledge. This techne was also often demonstrated in practice, through the so-called "epideixis", a public display of knowledge. This was especially common in the crafts, but also and especially in medicine. However, a public display of mathematical facts was unthinkable in ancient Greece – the reason for this obviously lies in the special ideographic notation mentioned above, which can only be grasped with a certain degree of prior knowledge and was therefore not accessible to the general public.

5.1 Logic and Knowledge: Symbolic Representation

We had already highlighted the importance of discourse in ancient Greece. So it is not surprising that the study of discourse was an important discipline of the philosophers. Aristotle had also studied it, and through this work is considered one of the co-founders of the scientific discipline of logic. In the following, we want to trace the arc from Aristotelian logic to a form of logical knowledge representation that is common in AI research today.

Aristotle

introduced logical rules of inference, the syllogisms, to describe the process of reasoning. We have already mentioned that mathematics in Aristotle's time had already produced formal notations and proofs; Aristotle was well aware of these disciplines and results. He was, however, concerned with formalizing discourse; conclusive chains of reasoning were to be recognized and separated from false ones. He was particularly concerned with avoiding false conclusions; he was well aware that a conclusive chain of evidence does not yet say anything about the substantive correctness of the result – for this the premises used would also have to be true.

The following example of a syllogism has two premises, these are the statements above the line, which say something about all men and about Socrates. The deduction rule, the syllogism, now allows us to deduce a conclusion from these two premises – this is the statement below the line.

$$\frac{\text{All humans are mortal.} \qquad \text{Sokrates is human.}}{\text{Socrates is mortal.}}$$

This conclusion is correct, and it is correct regardless of the truth of the two premises. Let's change the first premise a little by changing "mortal" to "immortal":

$$\frac{\text{All humans are immortal.} \qquad \text{Sokrates is human.}}{\text{Socrates is immortal.}}$$

We again get a correct conclusion, even if we are aware that a premise does not correspond to reality. By this simple example it should be clear that this form of logic is concerned with the formulation of valid reasoning and conclusions from basic propositions, also called axioms. One can then derive new true statements from a set of axioms that are assumed to be true through a chain of applications of syllogisms.

With this work, Aristotle laid the foundations for the type of logic in use today, namely predicate logic, a logic in which statements can be quantified. It would take until the nineteenth century, however, for the work of Gottlob Frege, a German mathematician and philosopher, to lay the foundations for applications of logic in mathematics. Until then, Aristotelian logic had played an important role in philosophy in various periods. In the scholasticism of the Middle Ages, the works of Aristotle were used to study proof in mostly theological questions. However, the Catalan philosopher Ramon Llull stands out from this period, working to construct a "logical machine" as early as the thirteenth century. Various discs containing terms and logical operators could be rotated around a center, thereby mechanizing the syllogistic rules of deduction – a very early and modern form of automatic logical reasoning. This work was well known to seventeenth century Enlightenment philosophers such as Descartes and Leibniz, and certainly influenced their research.

Enlightenment

We have already spoken about the role of the Enlightenment in Chap. 3 on body and mind. The argument "cogito ergo sum" placed thinking, of course rational thinking, at the centre of being human. The German polymath Gottfried Wilhelm Leibniz went one step further by being convinced that all concepts or terms can be represented as numbers.

This would also make them accessible to mathematics, so that instead of arguing or discussing, one could simply calculate. His vision was, after all, that philosophers would no longer discuss, but only calculate with each other. In fact, Leibniz also helped design the foundations for such a program. Among many concepts from philosophy, mathematics and jurisprudence, Leibniz is considered the founder of the dual number system on which today's computers are based. He had also designed a mechanical calculating machine, although it is unclear whether he was able to build it as a working machine with the tools of his time.

Here we see for the first time a use of logic that clearly goes beyond a propaedeutic character. Propaedeutics is understood as a kind of preparatory instruction for scientific work, and here logic is considered a general propaedeutics. The approach of bringing logic and mathematics together was most radically demonstrated in the so-called Hilbert program. David Hilbert was a leading German mathematician who worked in Göttingen at the turn of the twentieth century. In the 1920s, Hilbert had proposed a research program that aimed to define mathematics as a formal system. In this system it should become possible to prove all mathematical theorems and thus establish their validity beyond doubt. At that time Hilbert was already a world-famous mathematician, so that his ideas also received widespread attention. At this time the work "Principia Mathematica" by Bertrand Russell and Alfred North Whitehead was written. In this three-volume study, an attempt was made to redefine mathematics in a formal logical framework precisely in the spirit of Hilbert's program. To do this, the authors also used the aforementioned development of Gottlob Frege's logic. Many notable mathematicians and logicians participated in the attempts of Hilbert's program until a young Austrian graduate student, Kurt Gödel, showed that it is impossible to formalize all of mathematics in such a way that all true statements are provable in a formal system. Thus, although in a strict sense Hilbert's program failed, nevertheless much research in this area laid the foundations for modern mathematics, and especially computer science. This is also the origin of the treatment of knowledge with the help of logic. Existing knowledge is represented by logical formulas, from which new formulas, new knowledge, can be derived with the help of rules of inference. Let us return to the example with which we explained syllogisms above. We now write the statements of premise and conclusion as a formula in the language of logic:

$$\frac{\forall x \big(\text{human}(x) \to \text{mortal}(x)\big) \qquad \text{human}(\text{socrates})}{\text{mortal}(\text{socrates})}$$

The symbol $\forall$ stands for "for all" and $\to$ for "implied". The first premise thus reads "for all objects x, if x is human, x is also mortal". With the help of the rule of inference, the new knowledge, namely that Socrates is mortal, can thus be derived from the two premises. This example also makes it clear that we are dealing here with the formulation of knowledge about the world and not with mathematical facts. This use of logic, i.e. for the representation and derivation of knowledge, was also particularly advanced by the new discipline of artificial intelligence in the 1950s.

5.2 Cognitive Revolution

AI research had established itself under this name at the Dartmouth Conference in the summer of 1956 in the USA. From the beginning, the automation of logic played a central role. Attempts were made to solve problems in highly simplified environments using knowledge represented by logical formulas. This included puzzles, games like chess or mathematical problems. On the other hand, the processing and translation of natural language texts were also an important sub-discipline of AI. Understanding texts and stories requires not only linguistic knowledge, but the reader must also have general knowledge about the world and the domain of the text. If an AI system is to understand and deal with a text, this knowledge must be in formalized form. Thus, it is not surprising that the first approaches to formulate general world knowledge came from linguistics. Linguistics also played an important role in the context of the "cognitive revolution" and the emergence of cognitive science. In 1959, the linguist Noam Chomsky wrote a critique of the work "Verbal Behaviour" by the then leading representative of behaviourism in psychology, B. F. Skinner [1]. In it, Chomsky criticized Skinner's approach to language as learned behavior, and subsequently became one of the co-founders of cognitive science. Chomsky later also became known for his approach to structural linguistics, which also laid the foundations for the development of programming languages for computers. Chomsky is discussed in more detail in Chap. 12. Also, the then emerging information theory and first computers were used by cognitive scientists to actually model. Behaviorism, which had been influential up to this time, had conceived of the brain as a closed unit, a black box. What had interested was its functionality, its behavior. In contrast, cognitive science now tries to understand the inside of the box. The computer as a tool offers the possibility to model and simulate it.

Starting from a work on semantic knowledge by Ross Quillian [2], the concept of semantic networks has spread in AI. The idea of representing knowledge in network form can also be found earlier, e.g., to model how people associate. As an example, consider the network in Fig. 5.1, where concepts are represented as boxes, and the arrows have the meaning "is subconcept of". For example, mammal is a subconcept of creature, expressing that every mammal is also a creature. The dashed line from Socrates to the concept Man expresses that Socrates is an instance of the concept Man. Thus, by virtue of the sub-concept relation in the net, he is also a mammal and a living being. Attached to the concept mammal is a so-called role, this is a property that applies to all individuals of the concept: all mammals have a lung. The special

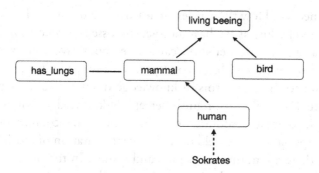

Fig. 5.1 Semantic network with the concepts living being, bird, mammal and human. Socrates is an instance of human, and mammals have lungs

feature of such semantic networks is that they allow the inheritance of roles. The elements of a sub-concept inherit all roles of the super-concept. So humans have a lung, and of course this is also true for Socrates, since he is human.

Until the 1990s, semantic networks were a widely used paradigm for the representation of knowledge in artificial intelligent systems. But they were also popular in the cognitive sciences and psychology as a model for the mental representation of knowledge. If one assumes that knowledge is stored in the brain in network form, one could explain associations that we humans are capable of making by structural similarities of different subnetworks. The German psychologist Klix tried to prove by experiments that networks are the basis of mental representation in humans. He was able to show that the reaction times of test persons to questions concerning concepts that were close to each other were shorter than those of concepts that were further away from each other [3].

A widely used model by cognitive scientist Anderson, the ACT model, also uses semantic networks [4]. In this model, two different types of knowledge are represented. One is conceptual or meaning-based knowledge – our Fig. 5.1 is a simple example of this – but procedural knowledge is also modelled. Procedural knowledge is mostly acquired through lengthy learning processes; for example, we learned to walk more or less laboriously as infants, we acquired this ability through a learning process. We have already mentioned this above in connection with Bergson's theory. Here it is important to note that procedural knowledge cannot be learned by reading or studying conceptual descriptions. You can read all the books you want on hitting technique in tennis; without practice, you will never be able to produce a passable backhand stroke. In ACT, such procedures are stored by rules, which can then be executed as needed. How these rules are learned is a question that needs to be studied separately. Just as we have not yet discussed how conceptual knowledge, such as a semantic network, can come about. We will examine such questions in connection with the concept of creativity in Chap. 9.

In addition to the two forms of knowledge discussed so far – procedural and conceptual – we also distinguish perceptual knowledge. For example, we have memories of images, sounds, or smells that we can recognize and describe or rewrite. Especially in the field of mental representation of spatial, pictorial knowledge, there are numerous studies and results. In the meantime we can be sure that in the human brain knowledge is also stored pictorially, i.e. in analogue and not in symbolic form. For this you can subject yourself to a simple self-experiment: Please consider now how many windows your apartment or house has ….

Stop, please don't read any further! Try to answer the question first.

… and now please observe how you gather this information. You have probably just walked through the individual rooms of your apartment in your mind and counted the windows. This is an indication that a picture of your apartment exists in your brain and that you can actually draw conclusions from this picture. There are numerous sophisticated experiments in cognitive psychology that prove this, and of course the processing of spatial knowledge is also the subject of AI research.

5.3   The Heyday of AI

In the 1980s, AI attracted particular attention through the so-called expert systems. These are software systems that were able to demonstrate the performance of human experts in a narrow field. These included systems such as MYCIN for diagnosing bacterial infections or DENDRAL for identifying chemical structures using mass spectrometer data. What all these systems have in common is that they must have a great deal of knowledge in the respective field. Part of the software must therefore be an extensive knowledge base in which the expert knowledge is formulated in such a way that it can be automatically processed by the computer. The semantic networks discussed above are very well suited for exactly this purpose. On this basis, a variety of formalisms emerged that were used for the design of knowledge bases. Such systems had complex and powerful methods for retrieving knowledge and relating it to each other. A weakness of these methods was seen by some critics in the large number of different language constructs that came to be used. Even our simple example in Fig. 5.1 has three different connecting lines: arrow, dashed arrow, and undirected line. In some cases, the meaning of these constructions was also not specified precisely enough, so that the algorithms used were also not always clear and understandable.

Thus, there were heated discussions in AI at this time about which formalisms were better suited for the representation of declarative, i.e. conceptual, knowledge. On the one hand, logicians in particular cited for their logic-based languages the clear semantics that had been studied for centuries and the sophisticated methods for deriving new knowledge. Using Aristotelian syllogisms, we had already studied this formal derivation. On the other hand, proponents of net-based languages argued that their systems were probably closer to the human mental representation of knowledge. However, this discussion died down rather quickly. Namely, in the early 1990s, when it became clear that semantic networks are nothing more than graphically represented logical formulas. Very quickly, systems were established that used logic and the usual derivation mechanisms. In the meantime, the use of so-called "description logics" has become standard; our example from Fig. 5.1 reads as follows in such a logic:

$$
\begin{aligned}
\text{human} &\sqsubseteq \text{mammal} \\
\text{mammal} &\sqsubseteq \text{living\_beeing} \sqcap \exists \text{has\_lung.Thing} \\
\text{bird} &\sqsubseteq \text{living\_beeing} \\
&\text{human(Sokrates)}
\end{aligned}
$$

Here, similar to the arrow in the semantic net, the symbol expresses the subconcept relation, so in the first line that all humans are also mammals. The second line is a bit more complex, in addition to expressing the subconcept relation, it also expresses in a logical form the role has_lung from our semantic net. The line states that mammal is a subconcept of the concept described by the expression to the right of the symbol: this concept is defined by two parts linked by a conjunction, the symbol $\sqcap$. In the first part it is specified that it is a part of the concept living being and in the second part $\exists$has _ lung. Thing it is expressed that there is at least one object that is any concept Thing, which is called the lung of this living being. The last line expresses that Socrates is an individual of the concept human.

We have explained this small logic knowledge base in such detail in order to make it clear that the same facts are formalized here as in the graphic-oriented network representation about a small section of the world. Obviously, it is now the case that the graph, i.e. the semantic net, seems much more catchy and intuitively understandable. However, we had already emphasized several times that logical formulas are not only a propositional representation of knowledge, rather logic simultaneously and without additional programming, so to speak, offers procedures to infer new knowledge in a correct way. Thus we could ask the above knowledge base whether Socrates has a lung, which could indeed be answered automatically.

5.4   Cognitive Computing

At the beginning of this section we briefly discussed natural language texts for the representation of knowledge. We had argued, on the basis of the ancient Greek scriptura continua, that texts were then written to be read aloud in order to reproduce speeches. It was not until much later, in the Middle Ages, that word spacing and punctuation became established; this made it possible to read texts silently, which then allowed them to be used to represent knowledge. We are all very used to this and have been deriving our knowledge from such textual sources since our earliest school days. In the meantime, not only books but also digital media and digital reference books are extremely common. Now, we had further argued that natural language texts need to be read and interpreted by humans and therefore seem less suitable for artificial systems. This was also a main motivation in AI research for the development of symbolic and formal representation formats as we had presented them.

Two developments can be observed that change the situation: First, text passages on the Internet are often multi-modal, insofar as they contain machine-readable formal parts in addition to text. On the other hand, intelligent search in natural language texts has made enormous progress, of which any user of one of the usual search engines can easily convince himself.

For multimodality, we consider as an example Wikipedia, certainly the most widely used encyclopedia in the world. The entries in it contain, besides their text part (and of course images), a so-called Wikidata record. This dataset contains some formal descriptions of the text entry. For example, the record of the entry "Ulrich Furbach" has a record where it is stated that Furbach is an "instance of" the concept (here they are called classes) "human" and he has a role "occupation", which is of the concept "computer scientist". If we click on "human", we reach the corresponding dataset and we can see that "human" is a "subclass of" "person" and also a "subclass of" "omnivore". If we graph this information similarly to Fig. 5.1, it is immediately clear that this is a kind of semantic network for representing knowledge. However, as we discussed above, these are also just logical formulas; so we could now formally infer from this knowledge that Furbach is an individual of the class "omnivore".

Wikidata is therefore a kind of formal supplement to the textual content of Wikipedia. The aim is to provide knowledge that can be read and processed by computer programs. The Wikipedia entry of Wikidata [5] states:

"In 2013, IBM donated the 2013 Feigenbaum Prize prize money for the Watson project to the Wikimedia Foundation and, by name, Wikidata, because Wikipedia had been a major contributor to the project's success and Wikidata's goal was to provide easier access to knowledge for both people and machines."

In our context, it is important that access for machines is also explicitly mentioned here. Now this is not at all surprising if you know anything about the Watson project that won the prize. Watson is a software system developed by IBM to compete against human contestants on the quiz show Jeopardy! on US television. On Jeopardy!, players are presented with answers from a wide range of knowledge areas; the task is then to find the corresponding question. For example, the answer to "In order to marry Elizabeth, Prince Philip had to give up his claim to the crown of this southern European country" would be "Greece." In particular, the speed in which the answer is given also counts here. Since the questions can come from a wide variety of fields of knowledge, the participants must have a very broad general knowledge. But this is precisely the difficulty in designing knowledge-based computer systems. In 2011, IBM's Watson system – named after one of IBM's first presidents, Thomas John Watson – had beaten two human record holders to win the Jeopardy! quiz show. Watson didn't have Internet access to do this; all knowledge sources had to be available in the system. Essentially, Watson had text sources available for this along with formalized knowledge. Watson had to extract possible answer candidates from its knowledge base and then decide very quickly between the different answer candidates available for choice. In this process, the constant evaluation and assessment of one's own work and the answers found plays an important role. Here the question of the consciousness of such an artificial system formally suggests itself; in Chap. 11 we will discuss this in more detail.

Now there has already been a big bang in the computer vs. human competition, namely when the IBM system Deep Blue won against the then reigning world chess champion Garry Kasparov under competitive conditions in 1996. This was a tremendous achievement and greatly raised the public profile of AI research. However, if we now compare the tasks of Deep Blue and Watson, we immediately notice that chess is a fixed set of rules with a few rules and that the difficulty lies in the size of the search space resulting from the different move possibilities. Of course, knowledge also plays a certain role, since the computer has to know various openings and endgame strategies – but all this is incomparable to the amount of knowledge Watson has to process under very tight time conditions in Jeopardy!

In AI research, at the height of expert systems in the 1980s, there was the bon mot "It is much easier to simulate a professor than a crane operator." This was meant to express that specialized expert knowledge, such as a professor has in a narrow field of knowledge, can be made available to a computer in a formalized way much more easily than general knowledge and common sense, which a crane operator certainly needs for his work. In the following, the difficulty in dealing with general knowledge will be explained using an example from a test collection for AI systems: Together with a question, two alternatives are offered. The system must find out which is the more plausible alternative.

The man broke his toe. What was the reason for it?
Alternative 1: He had a hole in his sock.
Alternative 2: He dropped a hammer on his foot.

It is immediately clear to the human reader that the second alternative is plausible, and this despite the fact that neither "toe" nor "break" appear in the sentence. One must know that toes are part of the foot, that hammers are heavy, and that toes can break if something heavy falls on them. All this knowledge about fairly mundane things must be available to the computer and, just as importantly, it must recognize it as relevant and select it from its knowledge base.

The Watson system is an example of an AI system that can handle very large amounts of knowledge and also when the knowledge is presented in different forms – texts, images or formalized knowledge bases. IBM has introduced the term "cognitive computing" for such systems. The aim is to develop systems that cooperate with humans so that problems can be solved jointly that neither humans nor machines can solve alone. Example projects can currently be found in the field of medicine, especially cancer treatment, in finance and in education. One website features videos of Watson talking to tennis star Serena Williams about training plans or to Bob Dylan about his song lyrics. If such cognitive computer systems are to work with humans, it is surely also important to know how humans process knowledge and how humans are capable of remarkable memory feats in many cases. Take, for example, the ability to recognize faces. We can often recognize faces we saw long ago with incredible speed. But we are just as fast when it comes to interpreting facial expressions. Presumably, such memory and interpretive abilities are located in a part of the brain that is very old in terms of developmental history. After all, it was important for survival to distinguish friend from foe and, of course, to recognize and evaluate the emotional state of the other person.

5.5 Artificial Neural Networks

We had already talked about the cognitive revolution in the context of the beginnings of research on knowledge representation. The departure from a purely behaviorist view had led to thinking about the structure of memory. This period also saw the first reflections on the process of learning, i.e. on the acquisition of knowledge. Up to now we have discussed symbolic, logic-based representations of knowledge, whereby we had disregarded the acquisition of knowledge, i.e. learning. If we now try to reproduce the structure of the brain in order to represent knowledge in this artificial structure, symbols or names cannot be stored directly. We then speak of subsymbolic representation of knowledge, and we shall see that this representation is very closely associated with a learning process for the acquisition of knowledge.

Evidence of research into the structure of the brain goes back as far as ancient Egypt, where brain surgery was already performed to treat diseases. Likewise, numerous references to brain research can be found over the millennia. It was not until the microscope became a tool of neuroscience and sophisticated staining techniques were used that it became possible to identify individual neurons and their structure at the end of the nineteenth century. This made it possible to hypothesize that neurons are the functional units of the brain. Thus, in 1906, Camillo Golgi and Santiage Ramón y Cayal were awarded the Nobel Prize in Medicine for the work that led to this insight. At the same time, it was discovered that neurons can be stimulated by electricity and, more importantly, that the electrical state of a neuron influences neighbouring neurons.

An elongated cell projection, the axon, extends from a cell; the shorter cell projections are the so-called dendrites. Figure 5.2 shows a single neuron with its axons. With the help of the axons and dendrites, a cell structure, a neuronal network, can now be formed. A cell is connected to another cell via its axon. The axon has a branching at its end that connects to the dendrites of another cell. Excitation can now be transmitted from one cell to another via this connection. This connection is not rigid or fixed, but rather occurs via synapses that are present at the ends of the axons and the dendrites. The signal transmission at the synapses does not occur directly, but through chemical messengers that pass on the excitation; as a result, this connection can be altered – strengthened or weakened. This synaptic plasticity is the basis for the changes that are constantly going on in our brain. We remember, we forget, we learn; all of these are changes in the structure of the brain – we will look at this in more detail below. We have already explained how cells are connected to each other. Simplified, we can represent such a neural network as a graph

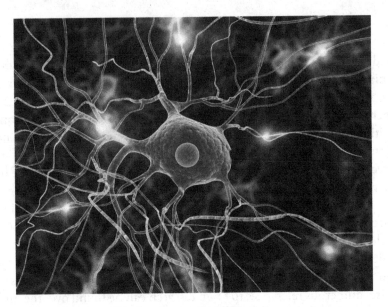

Fig. 5.2 Active nerve cell. (© Sebastian Kaulitzki/Fotolia)

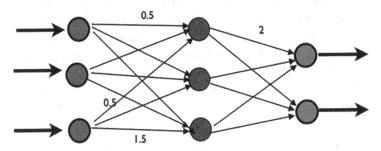

Fig. 5.3 Artificial neural network. The red nodes have input signals that are forwarded via the weighted edges. The green nodes are output nodes, which finally provide the output signals. Numbers on the edges mean that the signals along the edges are multiplied by this factor, i.e. amplified or attenuated

consisting of nodes and their connections to each other. Figure 5.3 shows a small toy example. Input signals are applied to the red nodes, which are forwarded via the weighted edges.

The green nodes are output nodes, which finally provide the output signals. Numbers on the edges mean that the signals along the edges are multiplied by this factor, i.e. amplified or attenuated. So what happens in each node when signals arrive? The computational capacity of a node is quite simple: it collects all incoming signals, adds them up, and if they exceed a given threshold, it passes the signal along the edge that leaves it. Consider the top green node in

Fig. 5.3: Three edges of each blue node reach it; the signal from the top blue node is multiplied by 2 and added to the signals from the other two blue nodes. Let us assume that each of the blue nodes sends the value 1; then our green node receives once the amplified value 2 and twice a 1, so in total the excitation potential 4. Depending on the threshold value of the nodes, a signal of the green output node is now sent. According to this scheme, calculations happen with the help of such an artificial neural network. Numerical values are available at the input nodes, and these are forwarded to the nodes of the next layer according to the weights at the outgoing edges; in our example, these are the three blue nodes of the middle layer. There, the values are summed up and forwarded to the nodes in the next layer; in the example, these are the two green nodes, which are also output nodes here and provide the result. One can now perhaps imagine that such networks can be used to perform complex calculations.

In Fig. 5.5 two very simple nets – each consisting of only a single node – are given, which compute the two logical connections and and or. These connections are important in that they are known to be sufficient, together with negation, to perform arbitrarily complex Boolean functions, i.e. functions over the truth values 0 and 1 – and this is exactly what computers do at the deepest bottom of their hardware.

Based on the neuroanatomical findings we explained at the beginning of this section, there were numerous approaches in the 1940s and 1950s to recreate neural networks by mathematical models quite in the style of our little example. Particularly well researched and relatively simple were the so-called perceptrons. Perceptrons consist of two layers of nodes, an input layer directly connected to the nodes of the output layer. In the example of Fig. 5.3, one would have to delete the blue nodes of the middle layer and connect the red input nodes directly to the green output nodes – one then obtains the perceptron of Fig. 5.4. The two nets in Fig. 5.5 also represent perceptrons; their only input node in each case is also an output node.

Now, such a network is not only able to calculate, it is also able to learn. For this purpose, an observation made by the psychologist Donald Olding Hebb in the 1940s can be used, which states that synaptic connections between neurons are strengthened when they are used frequently. Synaptic plasticity thus forms the neurophysiological basis of learning and memory. We will discuss the neurophysiological aspects in more detail in Chap. 9. Here we want to investigate how learning can proceed in the artificial neural network.

Assume that the perceptron in Fig. 5.4 is to learn to recognize images of a rose and to distinguish them from other images, i.e. a typical image recognition task. For this purpose, an image can be divided into individual image

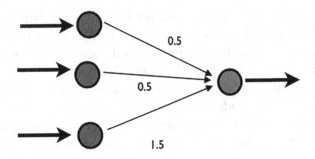

Fig. 5.4 Perceptron with three input nodes (red) and one output node (green)

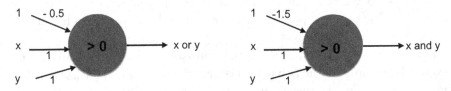

Fig. 5.5 Boolean functions. The upper edge with a fixed input value of 1 is called the bias. The weight on this edge can be used to modify the threshold of the neuron so that it can be set uniformly for all neurons, here >0. On the left, a single-neuron network for computing the Boolean function or. If x or y have the value 1, the neuron returns the value 1, otherwise 0. For example, if x = 0 and y = 1, the neuron reaches the value (1* - 0.5) + (1*0) + (1*1), so +0.5. Since 0.5 > 0 holds, the neuron fires and outputs the value 1. On the right, a one-neuron network for computing the Boolean function and. If x and y have the value 1, the neuron returns the value 1, otherwise 0

points, pixels, so that each pixel corresponds to a gray value. These gray values are now applied as numerical values to the inputs of the perceptron. Of course, this requires much more than the three input nodes in our toy example. If the image corresponds to a rose, the output value of the perceptron should be 1; if this is not the case, change the weights at the edges according to a given rule; do the same if the image is not a rose but the perceptron falsely claims it is. In this way, one gives the perceptron a set of learning examples, observes the result at the output node, and modifies the weights as needed. After all, such artificial neural networks are mathematical models that can also be studied with the help of mathematics. One can specify exactly under which circumstances a perceptron is able to learn a classifier (e.g. rose – or not rose). Once the classifier is learned, the artificial neural network can be used like a computer program – no further modification of the weights is required. The knowledge about the "essence of a rose" is in the network and the weights at the edges in the perceptron.

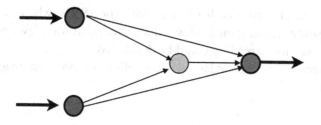

Fig. 5.6 Neural network with an inner hidden node

The idea of using guided learning to develop systems that can solve complex tasks, much like humans can, is obviously fascinating. The fields of application are manifold, ranging from image recognition to the classification of properties of logical formulas. Accordingly, neural network research boomed from the 1950s onwards. This boom was clearly curbed by a book by Marvon Minsky and Semour Papert; in "Perceptrons: an introduction to computational geometry" [6], the authors examine in detail properties and limitations of perceptrons. One result is that perceptrons cannot compute the Boolean function *xor*, that is, an exclusive or. Figure 5.5 gives a network for computing an or. With such an or, at least one of the two input values must be true, i.e., 1, for the result to be a 1. In the case of *xor*, exactly one input value must be 1 – not both – for 1 to be output.[1] To compute an exclusive or, one needs a network that has at least one hidden node. Figure 5.6 shows the structure of such a network. As in the case of the perceptron, we have two input nodes (red in the figure) and one output node (green in the figure); in addition, however, there is also the inner yellow node, which does not return any value to the outside.

Designing a learning procedure for such a multilayer network is much more difficult than in the case of the perceptron. We had realized learning by observing the error at the output and modifying the weights. If we want to apply this procedure in the case of multilayer nets, the inner nodes pose a problem. In our example we do not know what the output of the inner yellow node should be – we cannot detect the error at its output in order to change the weights of its incoming edges. We can only observe the error at the output node.

The situation at that time, after the publication of Minsky and Papert's book, was that efficient learning methods were known for perceptrons, but at the same time it was clear that perceptrons were not sufficient to solve certain classification problems. This negative result greatly slowed down research in

---

[1] Very often in colloquial language or is used when an exclusive or is meant.

the field of neural networks. It was not until the 1980s, when the so-called backpropagation learning method was developed, that multilayer neural networks with learning capability could be developed.

We will revisit this concept later when we discuss vision and image processing in Chap. 7.

References

1. Chomsky N (1959) Verbal behavior. Language 35:26–58
2. Quillian MR (1967) Word concepts: a theory and simulation of some basic semantic capabilities. Behav Sci 12(5):410–430
3. Klix F (1984) Gedächtnis. Wissensnutzung. VEB Deutscher Verlag der Wiss, Wissen
4. Anderson JR (1996) Act: a simple theory of complex cognition. Am Psychol 51(4):355–365
5. Wikipedia (2015) Wikidata – Wikipedia, Die freie Enzyklopädie. (Online; Stand 24. Februar 2016)
6. Minsky M, Papert S (1969) Perceptrons. An introduction to computational geometry. MIT Press, Cambridge

6

Mnemonics

Abstract Tricks for remembering things have been around since ancient times. The loci method is well known, i.e. learning contents are arranged in a certain structure, in a certain space (lat. Locus!), a certain path, a letter-number sequence. Forgetting content can also be done by detours. Since the Enlightenment, the trend has been more toward grasping content and away from memorization. We discuss various mnemonics in this chapter, limiting ourselves largely to techniques that humans use.

Immanuel Kant, one of the great German philosophers of the Enlightenment, was considered an extremely punctual person who strictly adhered to a regular daily routine. An important role was played by his long-time servant Martin Lampe, who was in Kant's service for 40 years. When Lampe was dismissed after such a long time, Kant found it difficult to get used to his new servant; Lampe was too closely associated with his daily routine. What survives is a note from Kant saying that the name of Lampe must now be completely forgotten. The question now arises whether it is possible to remember to forget something. Is it useful to make a note to forget something?

In the previous chapters we have concentrated on storing and remembering or retrieving knowledge. Forgetting has not played a role so far. On the other hand, remembering and forgetting are two common antonyms – in our times of the ubiquitous internet and multiple social platforms, we experience that it is quite difficult to delete information, be it fake news or just embarrassing pictures, i.e. to make the internet forget. People have a much easier time of it.

© The Author(s), under exclusive license to Springer Fachmedien Wiesbaden GmbH, part of Springer Nature 2023
U. Barthelmeß, U. Furbach, *A Different Look at Artificial Intelligence*, https://doi.org/10.1007/978-3-658-38474-6_6

Harald Weinrich has written a wonderful book about this: "Lethe – Kunst und Kritik des Vergessens" [1]. In Greek mythology, Lethe is the goddess of forgetting – her counterpart is Mnemosyne, the goddess of memory. Lethe is also one of the rivers in the underworld; if one drinks of its waters before entering the realm of the dead, one cannot remember one's former life. Analogously, in the underworld there is also the river Mnemosyne; whoever drinks from this river becomes omniscient. Even in Greek mythology, remembering and forgetting are opposites that belong together.

Since ancient times, there have been numerous approaches and methods to remember and to fight against forgetting in certain situations. An episode from antiquity gives the poet Simonides of Keos as the inventor of the so-called loci method. According to this episode,[1] the poet Simonides, who was very famous at the time, is hired by the pugilist Skopas to write a song of praise for a victory he has won. Simonides writes these verses, but Kopas is dissatisfied because Simonides dedicates two-thirds of the song to the twin sporting gods Castor and Pollux and only one-third to the pugilist. Skopas then pays only one third of the fee, the missing part he should get from the gods. At the great feast that follows, Simonides is called to the door, two young men want to speak to him. When Simonides steps out of the hall, he finds no one there; at the same moment the ceiling of the room collapses, burying all the participants in the feast beneath it. All but Simonides are dead, so the gods Castor and Pollux have paid their debt to the poet. The collapsed ceiling disfigures the bodies beyond recognition, making them unidentifiable. Simonides, however, remembers the seating arrangement in the room and is thus able to identify the dead based on their position in the hall. Since that time, Simonides has been regarded as the inventor of mnemonics and in particular of the method that uses spatial structures as a mnemonic aid, the loci method (Latin locus "place", "location"). If you want to memorize a speech, for example, you select a well-known place in your mind, such as your own apartment, and then assign the individual parts of the speech to be memorized to the locations of the apartment in an orderly sequence. In order to remember, one then steps through the sequence of locations in the apartment, "recalling" the parts of the speech.

Also to forget, there is an episode from the same period: the politician and general Themistocles was a contemporary of Simonides. Themistocles was known for his good memory, supposedly knowing the names of all the citizens of Athens. When Simonides offered to teach Themistocles the art of

---

[1] Narrated here according to [1].

memory, the latter replied that he did not need the art of memory, he would rather learn to forget what he wanted to forget.

This also brings us back to Kant's note mentioned at the beginning. Is there a method to forget? Here, too, it is worth taking a look at antiquity, namely Rome, where the poet Ovid wrote about love in the early phase of his creative work. In addition to books in which he explains the art of love, he also described, as a counterpart, how to behave in heartbreak in order to forget a partner. The recipe from [2] is very simple; you remember as many negative aspects of your love as possible; if necessary, you can also talk yourself into it:

> Täusche dein Urtheil selbst; schmal ist die Grenze ja nur. Dick, wenn voll sie ist; wenn braun, magst schwarz du sie nennen; Bei der Schmächtigen kann Dürre man rechnen zur Schuld. Die nicht bäuerisch ist, die kannst leichtfertig du nennen; Bäurisch werde genannt Eine, die ehrlich und brav.[2]

Another technique is reported by the memory artist Solomon Shereshevsky. Russian neuropsychologist Alexander Romanovich Luria recorded this case in a detailed study [3]. Shereshevsky was a journalist and memory artist who performed publicly in the 1920s and achieved some notoriety. Luria diagnosed S. with a particularly severe form of synaesthesia; when he heard sounds he saw colours, when he touched he felt tastes, and so all his senses were more or less connected, and sensory impressions produced images in his mind. The spectacular feats of memory were possible with him through these images; he could memorize tables of numbers, complicated mathematical formulas, and even poems in a foreign language, and demonstrated this in his shows. However, his problem was not remembering, rather he managed not to forget. In between the multiple performances as a memory artist that he completed in one evening, he had to erase the images from each previous memory performance. Luria describes that in doing so, S. imagined that he placed an opaque film over these images and then crumpled it up in his hand and threw it away. He also took to writing content he wanted to forget on paper and then burning it – the going up in smoke was supposed to help him forget the content. Surprisingly, a much simpler method later proved effective: S. discovered that he could suppress the images by telling himself that he no longer

---

[2] Deceive thy judgment thyself; for the border is but narrow.
  Thick, if full she be; if brown, mayst thou call her black;
  With the slender one drought can be counted to blame.
  Which is not peasant, which can lightly call you;
  Be called one who is honest and well-behaved.

wanted to see them. This form of autosuggestion worked without Luria being able to find an explanation for this phenomenon.

Over the centuries, the art of memory, as it was described in antiquity as the loci method, was further developed and applied. In the process, the art also moved into the vicinity of magic. This means a kind of religious magic, through which one tries to get on the track of divine knowledge. The use of numbers and codes had something magical and was also used extensively in the Jewish secret science of Kabbalah. The Catalan philosopher Llulus, whose calculating template we had already mentioned in our treatment of knowledge representation in Chap. 5, attempted to gain access to divine knowledge through the magical combination of numbers. Giordano Bruno had also dealt with the art of memory in the sixteenth century, and when he lectured to Henry III about his writing on the art of memory, it can be assumed that Bruno certainly took advantage of the king's penchant for magic in order to convince him of his art [4].

Also in the Renaissance, Lambert Schenkel became famous with his writing "De Memoria". Schenkel had used a rather traditional loci method and toured with it through numerous countries of Central Europe. Descartes must have been aware of this writing, since he comments on it quite disparagingly in his Cogitationes privatae (1619–1621). He writes there (quoted after [1]):

> Als ich die anregenden Dummheiten des Lambert Schenkel las, habe ich mir überlegt, daß ich wohl alles das, was ich je entdeckt habe, mit meiner Vorstellungskraft umfassen könnte, wenn ich nur immer die Sachen auf ihre Ursachen zurückführte (*per reductionem rerum ad causas*). Und wenn diese dann schließlich noch auf eine einzige Ursache zurückgeführt werden, dann wird wohl klar, daß für die Wissenschaften insgesamt überhaupt kein Gedächtnis nötig ist (*patet nulla opus esse memoria ad scientas omnes.*)..."[3]

In this quotation a radical turn becomes clear, namely away from the art of memory towards rational thinking, towards reason. According to the motto "memorizing does not necessarily mean knowing", one rather tried to grasp things and then reproduce them when needed. It is no coincidence that the Age of Enlightenment also marks the beginning of formal logic; the German polymath Gottfried Wilhelm Leibniz had already designed mechanical calculating machines in the sixteenth century. At the beginning of the book,

---

[3] When I read the stimulating follies of Lambert Schenkel, I reflected that I could probably encompass all that I have ever discovered with my imagination, if I only always reduced things to their causes (*per reductionem rerum ad causas*). And if these were then finally traced back to a single cause, then it would probably become clear that no memory at all is necessary for the sciences as a whole (*patet nulla opus esse memoria ad scientas omnes.*).

we had already argued that the Enlightenment can be seen as a root of AI research. We are still working on methods for automatically deciding the truth of statements with the help of formal logics. In Chap. 5 we discussed in detail how knowledge is stored and processed in AI systems. We did not deal there with the problem of how memorized knowledge, once stored, is retrieved. In the field of information processing, however, this is a central issue: whenever we use a search engine like Google or Bing on the Internet, we face the problem of finding the entered search terms in the huge amount of web pages. For example, if we enter the keyword "knowledge" in Google, this search engine returns 248 million results in 0.72 s, which are then presented according to a certain ranking. One can imagine that sophisticated techniques have to be applied here to sift through the internet. However, this is not so much a matter of retrieving knowledge, of remembering, but rather of searching for individual words in huge amounts of text presented on Internet pages all over the world. In complete contrast to the principles of logic and enlightenment, individual words are searched for and found here without semantics.

You might think that memorizing facts no longer matters in this age of ubiquitous computer technology. But even today there is a lively community of memory artists and memory athletes, and indeed the loci method, which we had learned about on our excursion to ancient Greece, is also very popular there. In Germany, there is a Society for Memory and Creativity Promotion e. V., which regularly organizes German championships in memory sports. In addition, there is also an association MemoryXL, which also organizes championships, but also seminars. On the web pages of this association successful memory sportsmen describe their techniques.[4] The world record holder Franz-Josef Schumeckers [5] reports that he usually uses the route method: He memorizes a route with prominent points, for example in his apartment, and then places the objects to be remembered at these points. He says that it is quite helpful to let his imagination run wild and make up little stories about it. Schumeckers describes how he memorizes the tomatoes from a long shopping list in a route: "I connect the tomatoes as the 4th point on my shopping list with my 4th route point, the stairs. An avalanche of tomatoes rolls down the stairs, and I try to run up to meet it. Quite a muddy affair." The important thing here is to come up with several different routes, as a route is not immediately reusable after use. The images have become lodged in the brain, so you have to let some time pass to reassign the route.

---

[4] www.memoryxl.de, accessed 02/20/2018.

A similarly creative approach can also be taken in the discipline of name recognition. Boris Nikolai Konrad, 2011 world champion in this discipline, describes how he was able to memorize the names of 201 faces within 15 min [6]. His technique is to convert the name of the person as quickly as possible into a visual image. He writes that you can now imagine, for example, that Mr. Miller who is perhaps standing in front of you in a suit and telling you his name, is now suddenly carrying a large, dusty flour sack into a mill – which is just what a miller does. When memorizing first names he also imagines pictures for the most common names, e.g. Gabi with a "Gabel" (fork), Frank in a "Schrank" (cupboard), Dieter in a "Mieder" (bodice), Andreas with a "Ananas" (pineapple).[5]

Obviously, pictures and stories around these pictures play an important role in mnemonics. But what now when it comes to remembering as many numbers as possible? This is also a category in memory sports – let's listen again to top athletes in this field. Gunther Karsten, world champion in memory in 2008, describes that he also remembers numbers through concepts or objects. One method is to code the numbers 0–9 by a letter. For example, 3 is an m because it has three dashes, or 4 is an r because it is the last letter of the word four. Now only terms for two-digit numbers need to be found and memorized. For example, the 33 becomes the term mum because of its two m's, the 43 becomes the term rum because of its r and m. In this way, one learns what is called a master system table that assigns a term to each of the 99 two-digit numbers. Karsten now describes that in order to remember a 100-digit number, he memorizes 50 terms for the 50 pairs of numbers from the master system table. To do this, he writes a short story for the 50 terms, which he then memorizes. Alternatively, he also uses the route method for longer sequences of numbers with several hundred digits. The terms from the master system table are then stored along the route.

Another, particularly abstract discipline is the memorization of binary numbers. This involves sequences of several hundred zeros and ones, e.g. 100,101,000,100 … The multiple world champion Cornelia Beddies (751 zeros and ones memorized in 5 min) gradually converts such a very abstract sequence into the route method: First, three binary numbers are each converted to a two-digit decimal number. The first three digits of the above sequence, i.e. 100, result in the number 4, which can now be processed into a term using the master system table as above. So for 100, because of the r for 4, this can result in a "Reh" (deer) . The "Reh" can now be linked to the subsequent images and terms using the route method. It is remarkable that even

---

[5] Similar sounding words are represented.

in this very abstract discipline, people can memorize successfully if they manage to attach semantics to the almost meaningless sequences. These can be single stories or spatial arrangements – in any case a rich context is established. It is not surprising that spatial relations play an important role here. In the course of its development, for example, the human brain has constantly specialized and optimized itself for movements and estimations in space. For survival it has always been important to estimate distances and movements of our counterpart, be it enemy or prey. In our daily communication with others, we are also used to dealing quickly and efficiently with spatial relations. It is not surprising, then, that we try to make tricky use of this ability for non-spatial tasks such as memorization. We will see later in Chap. 7, using the so-called Wason selection task, that the human brain also performs worse in other abstract tasks than in comparable tasks that contain more context from our daily lives. We will examine in detail how remembering can be explained on a neural level in Chap. 9.

6.1 Summary

Mnemonics as the art of remembering large amounts of facts has been portrayed all the way back to ancient times. It has been shown that the loci method is an important technique that has been mentioned again and again. This memorizing has also been related to information retrieval techniques such as those used by search engines on the Internet. Furthermore, we argued that the use of spatial relations can be used profitably for memorization because the human brain is developmentally very well prepared for processing spatial tasks.

References

1. Weinrich H (1997) Lethe – Kunst und Kritik des Vergessens. Beck, München
2. Ovid (1861) Chapter Ovid: Heilmittel der Liebe (Ovids Werke, Fünfter Theil). Wilhelm Engelmann, Leipzig
3. Luria AR (1968) The mind of a mnemonist. Basic Books, New York
4. Ulbrich H-J, Wolfram M (1994) Giordano Bruno: Dominikaner. Gelehrter. Königshausen & Neumann, Ketzer
5. Schumeckers F-J (2011) Grundlagen Gedächtnistraining. http://www.memoryxl. de/gedaechtnistraining/tipps-der-meister/grundlagen-gedaechtnistraining.html. Accessed on: 31. Okt. 2018
6. Konrad BN (2011) Namen merken. http://www.memoryxl.de/gedaechtnistraining/tipps-der-meister/namen-merken.html. Accessed on: 31. Okt. 2018

7

The Art of Seeing

Abstract When we look at something, we see more than the information provided by our eyes. We – i.e. our brain – interpret this information and develop ideas that we associate with what we see, we are biased. Artists broaden or change our view by putting common ideas into a new context, often influenced by scientific knowledge. Neurobiologists divide the visual process into processing steps that come from bottom-up (stimulus elements) and those that come from top-down (cognitive elements). In AI image processing, systems learn to follow analogue steps to classify a large set of images. In deep learning, artificial systems are trained to classify objects using vast databases of images in order to recognize them on new unseen images.

In "Historia naturalis" [1] Pliny reports of a contest between Zeuxis and Parrhasios: Zeuxis, in a contest with Parrhasius, painted grapes so true to nature that birds flew in to peck at them. Parrhasius then presented his rival with a painting of a linen curtain. When Zeuxis impatiently asked him to move the curtain aside so that he could see what he thought was behind it, Parrhasius was sure of victory because he had managed to deceive Zeuxis. The curtain, after all, was painted. A prime example of a trompe-l'Œil!

This anecdote comes to mind when I come across pictures or works of art that irritate some viewers: And this is supposed to be art? This happens, for example, with monochrome painting or when encountering a ready-made, an everyday object treated like a work of art or a part of it: Marcel Duchamps' Urinoir led the way. Some viewers sometimes feel taken for a ride by such exhibits, cheated out of what they expect from art.

© The Author(s), under exclusive license to Springer Fachmedien Wiesbaden GmbH, part of Springer Nature 2023

U. Barthelmeß, U. Furbach, *A Different Look at Artificial Intelligence*,
https://doi.org/10.1007/978-3-658-38474-6_7

Even as a teenager, I was amused with my girlfriend when we came across strange objects in an exhibition about contemporary art that had little to do with the traditional concept of art: Everyday objects, installations, wrapped things, games with optical effects, moving sculptures, olfactory compositions, collections of things strung together, movement games, etc. Now and then confusion could occur: E.g. there lay an umbrella, pieces of clothing covered with flyers about the art exhibition, next to it a validated entrance ticket! Hm, we walked around this presumed artifact, searching in vain for the sign that revealed the artist's name and the title of the work. Uncertain glances at other museum visitors got us nowhere. Someone had probably just put their things away for a short time! Outside, we enjoyed becoming artists ourselves with our new perspective, discovering works of art in many places, not to say composing them, by reinterpreting our perceptions.

An artist, thanks to his impartiality and possibly in a kind of absent-mindedness, had looked beyond the average person's horizon and seen things in a new, unprejudiced way, i.e. under an unusual aspect, and made this visible through his design, opened our eyes. We had thus seen something that was actually there, but which we perhaps did not want to or could not see and therefore initially remained closed to our gaze.

How does the artist succeed in making the invisible visible? How does he manage to bring inner expression to the outside, secret desires to the surface? What does seeing mean, or seeing things as they really are? Is that possible at all? What happens when a viewer lets an art object affect him. Eric Kandel dealt with these questions and realized: All seeing is interpreting. We see with the brain! This means that there are connections between the creation and effect of art with the biology of the brain. In the following, we start from Eric Kandel's presentation of viewing art and brain research together and then explain the process of seeing in the human brain and in AI systems.

7.1   Art as Mental Gymnastics

On the basis of cognitive psychology, brain research and knowledge about memory, Eric Kandel examines visual perception, feelings and neuronal reaction patterns in his work "Age of Knowledge" [2]. He is guided in his argumentation by a world-renowned art historian, Ernst Gombrich, who, due to his bridges to neighbouring disciplines, has considered art from many-sided aspects.

One of his reflections leads to the observation that the work of art is completed only in the observer, because the perceiving brain itself contributes to the invention of what is seen. Kandel adheres to Gombrich's view of art:

Kunst ist eine Institution, der wir uns immer dann zuwenden, wenn wir uns schockieren lassen wollen. Dieses Bedürfnis empfinden wir, weil wir spüren, dass ein gelegentlicher heilsamer Schock uns guttut. Sonst würden wir allzu leicht in einen Trott geraten und neuen Herausforderungen, die das Leben uns stellt, nicht mehr gewachsen sein. Die Kunst hat also, anders gesagt, die biologische Funktion einer Probe, eines Trainings in mentaler Gymnastik, das uns hilft, mit dem Unerwarteten umzugehen. (quoted from [2]).[1]

Fehler! Linkreferenz ungültig. Thus he is in the best neighborhood with Bergson's philosophy of life!

Eric Kandel first observes the "mental gymnastics" of artists using the example of Viennese modernism around 1900, draws parallels to the findings of Freud's depth psychology and, as a brain researcher, points to correlations with neurology in the present day.

Erich (later: Eric) Kandel was born in Vienna in 1929

as the second son of Hermann and Charlotte Kandel, operators of a toy shop. After the "Anschluss" of Austria to the German Reich, the anti-semitic riots become increasingly threatening. Erich's memories are permanently shaped by them, which, among other things, contributes to making him a specialist in human memory, as he writes in his autobiography "Auf der Suche nach dem Gedächtnis " [3].

The family emigrates to the United States, where Erich, as a successful student, he got an admission to the historical and literary faculty at Harvard University in Cambridge. He comes to his true vocation only in a roundabout way. When he comes into contact with psychoanalysts who belong to the Freud circle, he plans to become a psychoanalyst. In 1952 he enrolled in medical school in New York. After some time, however, he turned away from psychoanalysis and turned to basic biological research, where he was particularly fascinated by the structure and function of the human brain. With the aim of discovering the neurological basis of Freud's instance model (id, ego and superego), he embarked on the career of a neuroscientist.

In 1963 he was able to prove that nerve cells can learn and are the basis of learning. Today's common knowledge that knowledge and experience manifest themselves in long-term memory in connections of nerve cells was a groundbreaking discovery at the time. Kandel explored all this with the help of sea snails called Aplysia or sea hares. These snails can grow up to 75 cm long. They have brains with only 20,000 nerve cells, each of which is very large and can be seen with the naked eye. Kandel stimulated these nerve cells with electrical impulses and saw that multiple irritated pathways expanded through new connections.

(continued)

---

[1] Art is an institution we turn to whenever we want to be shocked. We feel this need because we sense that an occasional salutary shock is good for us. Otherwise, we would all too easily get into a rut and be unable to meet new challenges that life throws at us. Art, in other words, has the biological function of a rehearsal, a training in mental gymnastics that helps us to deal with the unexpected.

(continued)

It is the same in our brain: if we dial a telephone number very often, we learn it by heart over time. The numbers manifest themselves in certain connections of the nerve cells. Otherwise we forget them.

In 2000, together with the Swede Arvid Carlsson and the American Paul Greengard, he received the Nobel Prize for the discovery of a special protein, which makes it possible to store a memory in long-term memory. Thanks to Kandel, we know that our brain is malleable, that negative experiences can be "overwritten" by positive ones, that traumas can be overcome, because the brain changes its anatomy by growing new synapses. Various imaging methods can be used to detect changes in the brains of patients receiving psychotherapeutic treatment.

He documented the development of the modern, neurobiologically based science of the human mind, among other things, in his aforementioned autobiography, which was later also made into a film.

Six years later, in his book "Das Zeitalter der Erkenntnis" [2], he bridges the gap between mind and biology by revisiting the disciplines, or their themes and issues, of his earlier studies and bringing them together in a synthesis.

Kandel chooses turn-of-the-century Vienna for his study of the connection between art and the brain. Artists and scientists were able to exchange ideas and influence each other at the university, in the cafés and salons. The "temporary cultural capital" of Europe offered them an unusual degree of tolerance and openness and enabled a fruitful dialogue between the individual disciplines.

7.2   Interaction of Art and Science

Influence of Biological and Evolutionary Theory

Kandel pays particular attention to the portrait painting of Klimt, Kokoschka and Schiele, who were strongly influenced by scientific research, findings in biology and psychoanalysis. He sees a parallel in the Renaissance, whose artists benefited from knowledge of human anatomy. They succeeded in creating an amazingly plastic recreation of human bodies that seemed to come to life on canvas. The gift of capturing the three-dimensional world on a two-dimensional surface, while coming as close as possible to the truth, continued to dominate the art scene in subsequent years, but became less important when a seemingly superior competitor appeared on the scene: the camera. The artist's gaze turned away from the outer world and wandered to the inner, to the "multidimensional inner self and the unconscious," an area that was also at the center of biological, evolutionary, and psychological research of the time. The rules of traditional painting lost their validity. The external resemblance of an object to what was painted was no longer the main focus. New accents were set, new aspects and dimensions of the human being were expressed.

Klimt, for example, refrains from three-dimensionality in his two-dimensional painting "Adele Bloch" (Fig. 7.1). Added to this are the ornamental and exotic patterns on Adele's dress, which on closer inspection reveal that they are not simply decorative, but represent symbols of male and female cells: rectangular sperm cells and ovoid egg cells. Klimt, strongly influenced by Darwin, was fascinated by the structure of the cell. The seductive charisma of the figure is thus associated with its reproductive capacity.

A reference to biological testimony processes can be found in the picture "Danaë". Danaë, the princess of Argos, has been locked up in a tower by her

Fig. 7.1 Gustav Klimt: Adele Bloch-Bauer I. (© Fine Art Images/Heritage Images/picture-alliance)

father because he was promised by an oracle that his grandson will kill him. Zeus, who desired her, transformed himself into a golden rain to approach her. The image shows a woman lying in an embryonic position, immersed in herself; on the left, golden raindrops symbolize Zeus' sperm; on the right, early embryonic forms refer to conception.

Influence of Freudian Psychoanalysis

But it was not only biological and evolutionary insights that revolutionized the world at the turn of the century. The Viennese Medical School revealed sensational connections between mind, brain and the unconscious. It was recognized that all mental processes have a biological basis in the brain and mental illnesses are biological in nature, much of human behavior is irrational and based on unconscious mental processes. The latter observation was particularly the subject of investigation by Sigmund Freud, who first attempted to describe mental life using basic neurobiological concepts, and then developed a new psychology of the mind independent of biology. This shift is largely due to the discovery by his older colleague Josef Breuer that unconscious mental conflicts can cause psychiatric symptoms and that these symptoms can be cured or alleviated if their unconscious cause is made conscious to the patient. This is done in part with the aid of hypnosis, or the "talking cure," as Anna O., a famous patient of Breuer's who suffered from hysteria, expressed it. Since hypnosis brought unconscious feelings to light, but the patient could not remember them upon awakening, Freud developed a procedure to overcome the repression that pushed away painful memories (often sexual abuse), namely the procedure of free association or dream analysis in psychoanalytic therapy. Freud recognized a correlation between observable behavior (e.g., symptoms), psychoanalysis (mental representation of conscious and unconscious mental processes), and the brain (brain mechanisms of conscious and unconscious mental processes), but refrained from linking all three areas in his research in order to devote himself entirely to the mental processes between the ego (direct contact with the outside world), the id (seat of instinctual drives determined by the pleasure principle), and the superego (unconscious instance of moral values). Artists such as Arthur Schnitzler, Gustav Klimt, Oskar Kokoschka, and Egon Schiele, who were familiar with Freud's concept, also searched for the processes beneath the social surface of human behavior. Despite his appreciation for Freud's pioneering work, Kandel admits to certain shortcomings: he was late to regard the death drive (thanatos) as an independent drive on a par with Eros and was extremely ignorant about women's sexuality.

In contrast to Freud, who considered clitoral stimulation regressive and immature, Klimt's drawings emphasize the erotic self-confidence of women pleasuring themselves. Whereas in earlier works with similar motifs the women look at the viewer to include them in the shared sexual experience, as if in need of male completion, in Klimt's work the women are completely absorbed in themselves and refrain from eye contact with the viewer, who thus becomes a passive observer of a private act. Klimt not only placed the sexuality of women at the centre of his works; aggression, death and unconscious urges are also among his themes, which his successors Kokoschka and Schiele also dealt with, albeit each in their own unique way.

Kokoschka described himself as a psychological "can opener". Like Klimt, he was influenced by biology and psychoanalysis, plus the discovery of X-rays, which promised a perfect anatomical interior view of the body. Not only the inner view of the models, but also the painter's gaze and his emotions were to come to the fore, with which he turned away completely from decorative modes of representation and towards Expressionism. Scratches, thumbprints, unnatural colours, exaggeration in form and colour, elements of primitive art and caricature characterise his painting, which concentrated on portraits, as in his opinion these best reveal the psyche of the model and that of the painter. Gestures were also used as a means of expression, sometimes revealing more than facial features. He also ruthlessly revealed his own inner self, as shown by his famous self-portrait on the poster he designed for the art magazine "Der Sturm" in 1911, which testifies to radicalism.

In Egon Schiele's work, the deep psychological expression visualized through gestures is replaced by that of the entire body. His soul life, dominated by existential angst, his sexual despair, his vacillations between passion, ecstasy, fear and horror are acted out in unusual, theatrical poses, even contortions, which he rehearsed in front of the mirror. He often depicts sexual acts on himself or with others. The stylistic features of his paintings, apart from uncanny distortions and enlargements of individual body parts (predominantly eyes and hands), are the sombre, sometimes ghostly hues and the continuous lines, a refined form of "blind contour drawing" developed by Rodin. The Expressionist era in Vienna comes to an end with Schiele's early death, he died of pneumonia at the age of 28.

7.3   The Viewer in the Focus of Art History

The influence of scientific knowledge in the fields of biology and psychology on the art world of the time is obvious. Nevertheless, none of the artists and scientists who communicated with each other succeeded in recognizing the correlations between art and science as such. Nor, according to Kandel, was this phenomenon made fruitful for a development of cognitive psychology. Only later would the reactions of viewers of art and the biological bases of unconscious feelings become the subject of research. This began in Vienna in 1930 and would continue to this day.

Freud's attempt to create a dialogue between art and psychology, while controversial, provided the impetus for the Viennese School of art history to develop a concept that placed the viewer of a work of art at the center. "Drawing in the viewing subject" called for an exploration of visual perception and emotional response. Thus the basis for a holistic cognitive psychology of art emerged.

Complex life experiences and conflicts influence the creation of images, which among other things also leads to them being ambiguous. According to Kandel, the ambiguity of the image triggers both a conscious and an unconscious process of recognition in the viewer. The latter thus undergoes two processes of cognition: that of empathy, in order to lose himself in a painting, and that of abstraction, in that he distances himself from his everyday life in order to follow the symbolic language of forms and colours. Two fundamentally new ideas through Gestalt psychology complement this approach, namely that the whole is greater than the sum of its parts and that our ability to recognize these relationships – to evaluate sensory information holistically and assign meaning to it – is largely innate. When we see a flock of geese, we perceive them as a unit rather than as individual birds.

The important innate principles of Gestalt psychology are to be applied to the lower levels of visual perception, that is, to the bottom-up processing of visual stimuli. Top-down perception, which takes place at a higher level, also takes into account learned knowledge, hypothesis testing, and goals that are not a priori integrated into the brain's developmental program. The brain's perceptual replication of an image is bifurcated – into projection, which reflects the unconscious, automatic rules wired into the brain that govern our vision, and inference, or our knowledge, which is based in part on inference and can be both conscious and unconscious [2]. Thus, there is an amazing parallelism between the creativity of scientific processes and the inferential creative generation of models by artists and the recipients of art. Influencing the viewer through a top-down process shows that there is no "innocent eye". When we see, we classify concepts and interpret visual information. If the brain relied only on the information it receives from the eyes, vision would be impossible. Access to the world is therefore only an illusion of the brain.

How does this happen in detail? How can vision be modeled in an artificial system?

7.4   Images in the Brain and in AI

We had talked about neural networks and their modeling in AI in detail under the aspect of knowledge processing and learning. Here we want to focus on the processing of visual information. We will start with the neurobiology of vision, then turn to technology in AI systems, and finally return to the amazing power of the human brain.

Neurobiological Aspects of Perception

Let's take an image that is being viewed: This image emits photons of light that strike the retina of the eye. There are specialized nerve cells, the photoreceptors, which react to the color, intensity and location of the light source. Two different types of receptors are distinguished here, namely cones and rods. Cones are sensitive to contrast and color. They are active in bright light and can perceive fine detail; they are located in the centre of the retina in great density and are extremely relevant to the visual discrimination of faces, objects and colours. Kandel argues that color vision is highly subjective and, moreover, very closely coupled to an observer's emotions. This could be one of the reasons why a painting can be perceived in different ways by different viewers. Rod cells are increasingly located in the outer regions of the retina; they are very sensitive to light and thus specialized for night vision. They are also responsible for capturing holistic elements of an image. Kandel illustrates this beautifully with the example of Leonardo da Vinci's Mona Lisa. This painting is generally regarded as an example of ambiguity in painting: the face sometimes appears smiling and radiant, the next moment wistful and sad again. One explanation for this changing perception could be that it depends on the way we look at it. If you look directly at the mouth, you perceive this part of the face mainly through the cones in the retina; these focus on the details of the mouth area, which means that no smile is visible. If, on the other hand, one looks at Mona Lisa's cheeks or hair, the mouth region is perceived by the rods in the outer region of the retina, which cannot see the details, but allow a holistic analysis. This brings out the smile.

So how is the information obtained by rods and cones transmitted? We have described in Chap. 5 on knowledge representation how information is transmitted within a network of nerve cells. In the same way, the transmission of image information to the other parts of the brain is now carried out by so-called ganglion cells. The axons of all ganglion cells group together to form the optic nerve, which leaves the eyeball and transports the information to the brain, more precisely, to the lateral popliteal tubercle, which is a part of the thalamus. From there, it is further conveyed to the visual cortex. At this point, an important processing step already takes place: the image is not simply reproduced, rather individual lines are extracted from the image. These lines can be recognized by strong contrast changes, i.e. by the border between light and dark areas of the image. However, the orientation of the lines is also detected, which then allows individual regions to be identified. A completion of lines also takes place here, which can be very helpful in object recognition, namely when objects are partially obscured by others.

In a further processing level, the individual lines of the image are now combined to form objects. In the process, the objects are separated from the background of the image. If one imagines a complex scene, one can certainly guess how elaborate these processes can become – a multitude of lines must be recognized, joined together to form contours, and finally the individual objects must be identified and isolated from the rest of the image. This part of the visual process described so far occurs through the bottom-up processes already mentioned above; processing steps that thus extend from the bottom, coming from the individual pixels, to object recognition. This part of the image processing runs unconsciously, we cannot observe or influence these processing steps voluntarily.

The further part of the viewing process is now based on memories, knowledge and on inferences; this can happen unconsciously or also consciously. The individual objects that are the result of the bottom-up processing are now classified in the top-down process, related to each other and linked to our memories. For example, we recognize a cat in the picture and can distinguish it very well from the dog that may be in the same scene.

Before we come to the special significance of face recognition in this level of the visual process, the procedure of AI systems should now be described. Image processing is one of the areas that has always been considered a central issue in AI research. The approach was traditionally guided by the findings of biology and neuroanatomy; the bottom-up process as described above was followed. In this process, the individual steps, such as line and contour recognition, were implemented by algorithms that used complex mathematical procedures. Images to be processed by an AI system are given as a grid of numerical values. These numbers express gray or color values and brightness. For example, the edges in an image can be determined by a mathematical operation on these number values, the Laplace filter.[2] We will not go into such traditional image processing methods here; rather, we will describe the procedure using so-called deep learning.

Image Processing in AI

Artificial neural networks, which consist of several layers of neurons, have already been introduced in the chapter about representation and reasoning (Chap. 5). We had emphasized that the inner layers of such a network are extremely important for the processing of signals and especially for the learning process, but on the other hand they also make the procedures very complex. In recent years, hardware and software have developed immensely, so that networks with several inner layers of neurons can now be trained efficiently. The AlphaGo system (cf. Chap. 2) uses two different networks, each with thirteen layers of neurons. Meanwhile, such networks can classify images better than humans. In a seminal paper on the subject [4], the authors describe their neural network as consisting of five convolutional layers (which we will explain in a moment) and three conventional layers composed of a total of 650,000 neurons. The task for this network was now to classify objects from Imagenet,[3] an image database that currently contains approximately 14 million images. The images in Imagenet are already classified, so it is very easy to test how correctly an artificial system has learned to recognize the objects in the images. The authors trained their system with 1.2 million images, just as we described in Chap. 5. This training process took a full six days; afterwards, using images that the system had not seen during training, it was possible to check what it had learned. The neural network had achieved an error rate of 17%.[4] Development has continued rapidly since these results were published: In the meantime, deep learning systems already achieve error rates below 5% and are thus more successful in classifying Imagenet images than humans.

Further above we had mentioned the so-called convolutive layers of the neural network. One can imagine such a layer as a small window that moves over the image. The image is given as a grid of numerical values for the gray or color values, and now all values in this window are calculated to a single

---

[2] Here the image is filtered by calculating the second derivative of the luminance function and then taking the zero crossings of this derivative as edges.

[3] http://www.image-net.org accessed 08/13/2017.

[4] Each image has five probable classifications at Imagenet. For example, if the image shows a leopard, snow leopard and jaguar are also possible classifications. The error rate indicates how many of the images were detected with a class that was not included among the five.

value. If this window is moved over the whole image and summarizes the values, you get a kind of compressed version of the image. The type of summary calculation of such a convolutive window is not fixed, but is modified and learned during the entire learning process of the neural network. It has been shown that a convolutive layer can be used to learn certain aspects of an image; these are exactly like the aspects of the bottom-up process of vision in humans, namely lines of different orientation or individual regions which are then characteristic of a face, for example. This process is called feature extraction.

It is particularly interesting because usually, when learning with neural networks, one does not know anything about what has been learned: the system can recognize an object after training with a certain error rate, but what has been stored in the neural connections is not accessible to a symbolic interpretation by humans. The learned knowledge is distributed over weights throughout the network. Through convolutive deep learning networks, it is now possible for the first time to identify individual aspects, features, of the image in specific layers of the network and represent them graphically. So far, such identification of learned knowledge has only succeeded in image processing problems, but of course the hope is high to be able to apply this approach to other learning and classification problems as well.

So far, we have come to know deep neural networks as an extremely powerful tool for image processing, but their triumphant march also extends into many other fields. When it comes to understanding spoken language, i.e. when we talk to our smartphone or our smart home device from Amazon or Google, learning processes with neural networks play a central role. Translating any language into another is now possible for free over the Internet, again thanks to neural networks. In Chap. 12 we will discuss language translation in more detail.

So it seems that Deep Learning with neural networks is a very universally applicable tool with great impact. However, there is a small fly in the ointment: Let's go back to image processing; there we talked about success rates that surpass humans when classifying Imagenet images. Unlike humans, however, deep learning network classification can be tricked quite easily, as Ahn Nguen and his co-authors recently demonstrated impressively [5]. Instead of giving images from an image database to the system for classification, they now classified their own artificially generated images. For this purpose, so-called genetic algorithms were used to generate more or less random images as patterns of dots. These images were then presented to the neural network for classification. After that, the images with the best classification value for some object were selected. Similar to what Darwinian evolution does, new images are now generated from existing images and random changes (mutations) are also made. These new images are now classified again and the process is repeated until finally images are produced that have been classified with over 99% accuracy. Figure 7.2 shows some examples of artificially generated images, all of which have been classified accurately. These are referred to as "false positive results"; a very impressive example is the image of a school bus (which in the USA are usually black and yellow) or a monarch. Of course, there are also generated images that we humans would classify in the same way as the neural network; Fig. 7.3 shows some examples.

The examples with the wrongly classified images show that the neural network has learned other criteria for classification than those that we humans use as a basis. Under these criteria, the network classifies the yellow and black

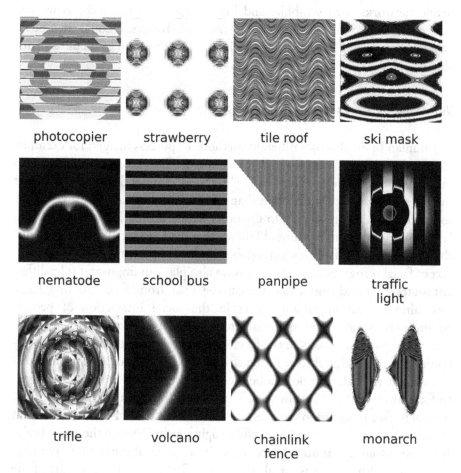

Fig. 7.2 False positives from [5]

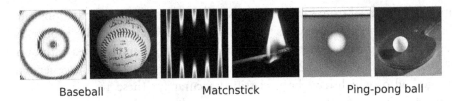

Baseball   Matchstick   Ping-pong ball

Fig. 7.3 Generated images and real objects from [5]

stripe pattern as a school bus with the highest degree of certainty. Of course, humans also make mistakes in this kind of classification task; here, however, the system considers its results to be almost absolutely correct. Some AI researchers criticize this approach of implementing AI exclusively with machine learning and neural networks. Instead, they call for a combination of neural networks with symbolic and knowledge-based methods, as we discussed in Chap. 5 on knowledge representation. The result could then be AI systems that are able to justify their decisions – we then also speak of "explainable AI".

What We Can Learn from the Brain

The human brain also uses different methods to process images; for example, faces and body parts receive separate treatments. The recognition of faces is a mechanism that develops from early childhood. Kandel describes in [2] that infants see faces much more often than other images and also learn very early to imitate facial expressions. On the other hand, already Darwin speculated, later this was taken up by Konrad Lorenz, that the large facial shape of infants, their eyes and roundish cheeks probably also evoke parental care. In the context of facial recognition, facial expression also plays an important role; different states of mind and emotions can be read from faces, so that facial recognition is an important aspect in the social interaction of people. Accordingly, various and quite different parts of the brain are involved. Individual parts or aspects of the face, such as nose, mouth and eyes, are recognized in the occipital lobe in the so-called occipital face area, in the fusiform face area in the temporal lobe these individual parts are then combined to form an overall view of the face. This area of the brain is arguably instrumental in face recognition and identification. All of this can be measured and visualized using modern and powerful imaging techniques on the active brain. It has been found that during face recognition, parts of the brain responsible for dealing with emotions are also activated. The amygdala, also part of the temporal lobe, is a developmentally ancient part of the brain; it is part of the limbic system, which is generally responsible for emotions and instinctive behavior. That emotions play an important role in face recognition is not very surprising; consider how quickly, when you first look at a face, you not only recognize whether it looks familiar, but you also immediately recognize whether the face has a friendly or aversive expression. As a counterexample, think of certain forms of autism where facial expressions are not recognized. Of course, face recognition is also coupled with other memory skills; after the first phase of recognition that we have just discussed, there follows the phase of activating memories associated with that face, and finally the name associated with the face also comes to mind.

The quick and often very reliable recognition of faces is sometimes in stark contrast to the search for the corresponding name. We immediately recognize that we know the face, perhaps also remember the context, but laboriously search our memory for the person's name. Such different performances are found in a wide variety of cognitive tasks and, surprisingly, emotion and intuition play an important role. And this even in tasks that look very rational at first sight. A very well-studied example is the Wason Selection Task, first studied by psychologist Peter Wason in 1968 [6]. The abstract case of the task is shown in the left part of Fig. 7.4. In the task, a subject is presented with four different cards. The subject is told that each card contains a letter on one side and a number on the opposite side. Further, a statement such as "If there is a vowel on one side, the opposite side contains an even number" is given. Now the subject is asked to verify or disprove this statement by turning over a minimum number of cards. In this abstract task, less than 25% of the subjects were able to find the solution; this result has since been confirmed many times with a wide variety of subjects. Even with students from logic lectures at universities, you get about the same poor results. It should be obvious (at least to a logician) that the statement "If there is a vowel on one side, the opposite side contains an even number" is formulated as a material implication "If P, then Q". Suppose that the property P holds, then Q must be true, but if P is false, then Q can be arbitrary. So in our case, we need to turn the card with A – here P is true, so we need to check if Q holds. Similarly, we need to turn the card

Fig. 7.4 The Wason Selection Task

with 5, because if there is a vowel on the other side, the implication would be false. A great many experiments have shown that people have problems correctly carrying out this abstract, yet quite simple, inference. The situation changes drastically when context is added to the problem.

In the right-hand part of Fig. 7.4, the context of a social contract is given: One side of the cards depicts a drink, namely beer or lemonade, and the other side depicts the age of the person drinking that drink. Thus, a card represents a person having a drink. The rule now is: "If a person is under 21 years old, he is not allowed to drink beer". What needs to be checked again is whether the implication, this time the social rule, is met. In this case, usually 75% of the subjects find the correct solution; quite quickly and effortlessly at that. This is, just as before, the checking of an implication "If P, then Q". However, now it is no longer in the abstract, but in a concrete social context, where it is a matter of checking a social norm. This apparently happens in a different part of the brain, namely the aforementioned, amygdala, which is responsible for emotions. A similar procedure is also found in another class of contexts, namely when it comes to precautions of the individual; i.e., contexts of the type "When you are in dangerous situation X, you must pay attention to Y." Tasks with such contexts are also processed in the amygdala. In [7], Valerie Stone and her co-authors describe experiments with a patient whose limbic system was injured, which also affected his amygdala. This patient was significantly worse at solving tasks involving social contracts than at tasks involving precautions. In the latter he was similarly poor as in the abstract case without context. From comparisons with healthy subjects and with other subjects with brain injuries, the authors clearly concluded that in tasks with the contexts addressed, other parts of the brain are used to solve the task. This is not done rationally, but with other developmentally very old and highly efficient working parts of the brain. How exactly this works and how it can be modeled in artificial systems is unclear and is being intensively researched in cognitive science.

7.5   Summary

Our observations show that it can be worthwhile to look beyond the boundaries of the disciplines. The different fields of science often shake hands, point to parallels, complement each other. We have discussed this using the example of the process of vision; in particular, we have taken as our starting point Eric Kandel's account of painting and science from Vienna at the beginning of the twentieth century. The painters of this epoch were certainly aware of the results of the natural and life sciences and incorporated them into their works. In the depiction of the visual process, we have noticed that on the one hand there are similarities between humans and AI systems, but on the other hand there is also a great deal that AI could still learn from humans.

It would therefore be downright absurd to forego the possibility of looking elsewhere for inspiration, because the complexity of our perception leaves its mark everywhere. So it is up to us to take off the blinkers now and then and open our eyes in order to open up new paths.

References

1. Cajus Plinius Secundus d. Ä, König R, Winkler G, Hopp J, Glöckner W (n.d.) Naturkunde / Naturalis historia libri XXXVII. Lateinisch-deutsch. De Gruyter, Berlin, Boston. Retrieved 8 Mar. 2019, from https://www.degruyter.com/view/serial/428834
2. Kandel E (2012) Das Zeitalter der Erkenntnis. Siedler, München
3. Kandel E (2006) Auf der Suche nach dem Gedächtnis. Siedler, München
4. Krizhevsky A, Sutskever I, Hinton GE (2012) Imagenet classification with deep convolutional neural networks. In: Pereira F, Burges CJC, Bottou L, Weinberger KQ (eds) Advances in neural information processing systems 25. Curran Associates Inc, New York, pp 1097–1105
5. Nguyen A, Yosinski J, Clune, J (2015) Deep neural networks are easily fooled: high confidence predictions for unrecognizable images. In Proceedings of the IEEE conference on computer vision and pattern recognition, pp 427–436
6. Wason PC (1968) Reasoning about a rule. Q J Exp Psychol 20(3):273–281
7. Stone VE, Cosmides L, Tooby J, Kroll N, Knight RT (2002) Selective impairment of reasoning about social exchange in a patient with bilateral limbic system damage. Proc Natl Acad Sci 99(17):11531–11536

8

Free Will

Abstract Free will of man is a prerequisite for planning, creativity and responsibility for his actions. Much is predetermined by the past, genetic imprinting
and social milieu. The question arises whether humans nevertheless have free
will or whether artificial systems can also be responsible. The latter plays a
special role in the field of autonomous vehicles. Bergson's concept of intuition
and the possibility derived from it of freely deciding between available memories is addressed, but also Libet's experiment, which suggests that humans do
not have free will.

*A breeze billows the curtains in barely perceptible gentle rhythms. The branches in
the tree sway just as gently, as if giving their solemn approval to everything. A
lurching butterfly mimes a falling leaf. Or is it one ...? No, he can't fool me. It is
not aiming at me, but rather at the bird fluttering excitedly in the branches,
which crosses the harmonious dance of the branches. Is he feeding his young? Is it
chasing away rivals? The trees pause for a moment, as if they need to reflect, until
the wind sets them swinging again. A cloud dims the light, abruptly dampening
the mood, placing a grave accent on the serene image for seconds. Involuntarily I
feel a slight shudder...*

*I weave my perceptions into a pattern, underlay causal connections, put my
humane stamp on them and that of my current state of mind. I cannot do otherwise. Tree, bird, butterfly, wind, cloud would have a completely different view
of things.*

© The Author(s), under exclusive license to Springer Fachmedien Wiesbaden GmbH, part
of Springer Nature 2023
U. Barthelmeß, U. Furbach, *A Different Look at Artificial Intelligence*,
https://doi.org/10.1007/978-3-658-38474-6_8

Much of what and how I see, think, feel, write, I owe to my education, my parents and the circumstances that brought them together and led them to beget me, and in turn their parents and the corresponding circumstances, and so on and so forth, all the way back to the origins of life in the first place, the Big Bang. When I think of how many possibilities were in play that could have prevented my existence, it almost makes me dizzy. I need only imagine what might have been had I not gone out on a certain night, had I not met this or that person who introduced me to another ... How many forks in the road there were that ultimately led to the emergence of a human being! Now, however, I am talking about one generation and me only. When I walk down the street and see how many people have had the same miracle happen to them, that they are there, when there could have been x number of ways that it could not have happened. What could have happened there! I would love to walk up to everyone and celebrate with them that we are there. "Yeah, you too, you made it. That was a close one! Man oh man!" And there we are, setting the course for future living beings, unaware of what step will have what consequences.

Pierre-Simon Laplace described the idea of determinism with all its consequences [1]:

> Wir müssen also den gegenwärtigen Zustand des Universums als Folge eines früheren Zustandes ansehen und als Ursache des Zustandes, der danach kommt. Eine Intelligenz, die in einem gegebenen Augenblick alle Kräfte kennt, mit denen die Welt begabt ist, und die gegenwärtige Lage der Gebilde, die sie zusammensetzen, und die überdies umfassend genug wäre, diese Kenntnisse der Analyse zu unterwerfen, würde in der gleichen Formel die Bewegungen der größten Him melskörper und die des leichtesten Atoms einbegreifen. Nichts wäre für sie ungewiss, Zukunft und Vergangenheit lägen klar vor ihren Augen.[1]

The question of the predetermination of our lives is crucial to the question of man's ability to learn, his responsibility for his actions and his ability to plan the future and to be creative. The questioning of free will is an extremely explosive topic and is discussed very controversially in various scientific fields. We would like to contribute to this discussion with a thought experiment: Admittedly, our present owes its existence to previously past events and actions. So a causal effect can be reconstructed retrospectively. For things have

---

[1] We must, therefore, regard the present state of the universe as the consequence of a former state, and as the cause of the state which comes after it. An intelligence, knowing at a given moment all the forces with which the world is endowed, and the present position of the entities which compose them, and which, moreover, would be comprehensive enough to subject this knowledge to analysis, would include in the same formula the movements of the largest celestial bodies and those of the lightest atom. Nothing would be uncertain for them; future and past would be clear before their eyes

happened as they have happened. Can it be deduced that they had to happen in such a way that alternatives were not in play? Can the future therefore be predicted? Does the experimental arrangement of "the world" as it is now permit precise predetermination, determinism, of all future events? Could one not expect that a small piece of the future could be reliably seen from the causal specifications of now-time? The results of quantum theory suggest that a consistent determinism within the physically tangible world is untenable. Within the framework of quantum mechanics, only probability statements about future observations are possible, which means that the spatiotemporal behavior of a microphysical system is fundamentally indeterminate. Chance also plays an essential role in modern evolutionary theory.

8.1 Free Will in Artificial Systems

Not only humans are affected by the question of free will. The following considerations show what implications the question of free will may have. In general, and especially in jurisprudence, it is assumed that humans have free will and are therefore responsible for their actions. In the context of computers, on the other hand, one often hears the opinion that the way a computer or a robot works is predetermined. Programmed by humans, the system does exactly what it is told to do. The software, the program, follows a huge if-then sequence of commands; all eventualities are provided for. Unfortunately – or rather, thankfully – AI systems do not work in this way; such systems have the ability to learn, and thus their behavior is unpredictable. For one thing, when the system is designed, the programmer does not yet know what external conditions, what sensory perceptions the system will have to learn from. For another, we saw in Chap. 5 that machine learning methods are relatively opaque, at least with respect to how they learned anything. Moreover, we could see from the examples in the field of image recognition how easily these systems can be fooled. So it is not at all predictable, what and how something is learned. It is true, that for every procedure can be stated, that it converges to an ideal behaviour under certain conditions; but these are statistical values, which predict a high reliability for very many runs. In individual cases, however, quite unpredictable results may occur. Such issues are also currently being discussed by politicians in the context of regulations for autonomous vehicles on public roads. The question here, in addition to general safety, is whether and how an autonomous vehicle will solve the so-called switch problem (trolley problem). This is an ethical and moral dilemma:

You are at the switch setting mechanism of a track system. A train is racing towards a switch, threatening to run over five people. When you throw the switch, the train moves to the other track, where it runs over one person.

How should the switchman decide? If he does not act, five people will be killed, if he acts and changes the switch, one person will be killed. Such or similar dilemmatic situations occur in a wide variety of fields, such as medicine or jurisprudence. Such issues have long been discussed in philosophy, and in particular two opposing views are found: a utilitarian view, according to which it is justifiable to sacrifice one life in order to save five, and an ethical and normative view, according to which the norm of not hurting anyone (i.e., not acting) is considered stronger than the norm of saving others (i.e., throwing the switch). So what course of action should be programmed into an autonomous vehicle in a situation comparable to the switch problem? The Federal Minister of Transport of Germany has appointed an Ethics Commission which issued a report on automated and connected driving in June 2017. This states quite clearly "Technical systems must be designed for accident avoidance, but cannot be standardized on a complex or intuitive accident consequence assessment in such a way that they could replace or anticipate the decision of a morally judgmental, responsible vehicle driver" [2]. Indeed, it does not seem feasible at present to formulate, and thus fix, ethical norms in such a way that they can be applied by an AI system in complex and diverse situations. We had already discussed in Chap. 5 how difficult it is to formalize and automatically process simple statements in which everyday and general knowledge is used. In the case of social norms, this is extremely difficult, and basic research on this is still in its infancy.[2] The complexity of the issues surrounding autonomous systems is also shown in another part of the Ethics Committee's report, namely when the topic of self-learning systems is addressed. This report is prefaced by a long list of requirements to be met by autonomous and connected vehicles. However, if an artificial system learns and thus develops further, it could well happen that it then behaves differently compared to its original state, i.e. before self-learning. The Ethics Committee avoids this problem by stating: "Given the current state of technology, the use of self-learning systems is therefore only conceivable for functions that are not directly relevant to safety."

[2] The authors are part of a research project Cognitive Reasoning, funded by the German Research Foundation: corg.hs-harz.de, accessed 27 July 2018.

8.2 Bergson's Intuition

We return to the human being and his existential circumstances and ask ourselves what dispositions him to be self-determined. We find a signpost in Bergson's concept of intuition. Bergson's intuitive approach may meet with rejection on account of the term intuition, since it sounds as if the philosopher lacks means of cognition and must swerve into the realm of the rationally unverifiable. However, Bergson's approach is anything but emotional or unscientific. By intuition he understands a methodical approach that conceives of man not only as a being of understanding, but also as a living being acting in nature. One of his premises is that a philosopher, free from prejudice, should take a simple yet profound look at man. The instrument of this direct vision of the mind he calls intuition. "Intuition accomplishes what intelligence never can: It brings us into the world as it is, without regard to utilitarian considerations." [3] He wants to devote himself to life as a whole, completely given, and not – like other positivist scientists committed to the scientistic worldview, with whose insights he was very familiar – to dissect it into individual experiences in order to then reassemble it: "Philosophizing is always a simple act. The more we allow ourselves to be penetrated by this truth, the more we will tend to liberate philosophy from the narrowness of orthodox science in order to bring it closer to life again." [3].

Bergson starts from the basic assumption that living beings have two instruments to fulfil their task in nature, instinct (predominantly in animals) and intelligence (predominantly in humans). In principle, Bergson argues, all living beings possess instinct or intelligence; there are only differences of degree in this regard; the two domains are not different in essence, just as the brain is not different in essence from the autonomic nervous system. Intelligence enables man to recognize, judge and compare matter and its relations. Its function is to count, weigh, measure and calculate, i.e. to make life easier with the help of technology. Bergson assigns this attribute of man to "Homo Faber". Intelligence is thus conscious, its tools are artificial, it is knowledge of form, while unconscious instinct means knowledge of matter or of a substance. The chief object of intelligence is the inorganic solid, life in parts, and the immobile, which it can dissect and put together.

Therefore, it is less suitable when it is to grasp living things. To supplement intelligence, man makes use of intuition. This has its roots in instinct, i.e. it has emerged from it. Intuition is the instinct that has become conscious of itself and reflects on its object. Intuition grasps life as a living whole and the duration (durée) of the individual. The insights gained through intuition, unlike the insights of the intellect, cannot be clearly expressed, but can only be examples or stimuli for arriving at similar intuitive insights. In this, the instrument of intuition does not exclude that of intelligence, for a philosophically fruitful use of intuition must also stand up to scrutiny by intelligence. Both forms of consciousness, intuition and intellect, complement each other; a sharp separation of the realms is not possible.

A brief excursion into literature may perhaps help to clarify the concepts: the protagonist in Max Frisch's novel "Homo Faber" fails in his life because he only acknowledges the rational side of man. He denies his creatureliness and rejects everything that can be attributed to it. He believes he can understand the world only through calculation and logic, and deceives himself by refusing to acknowledge intuition, which does manifest itself in him. On a ship he meets his daughter without knowing who she is, he falls in love with her, travels with her and sleeps with her. On a trip to Greece, she dies of a snakebite. He keeps a diary to account for himself, but even after realizing that he should have known – by intuition – who the young woman is, he resists admitting his error or wrongdoing.

Intuition, then, may be the key to what we call freedom, since it operates from the individual whole in the sense of durée and draws from the fund of stored experience or memory.

In cognitive science, intensive research is currently being conducted to learn why and how people solve some tasks quickly and fairly correctly, while other, often much simpler tasks can only be solved slowly and incorrectly. Intuition or gut feeling seems to play an important role in this. In Chap. 7 we had talked in detail about this phenomenon using the Wason selection task. Interestingly, these lines of thought are also supported from other branches of science. The neurobiologist Stefano Mancuso, for example, assumes that plants also have intelligence [4]; they just have very different sensory organs compared to humans, and they also communicate with each other in very different ways.

8.3   From the Categorical Imperative to the Free Choice of Memory

Immanuel Kant already pleaded for individual maturity in the Age of Enlightenment. Its – possible – path to individual freedom by intuition has been convincingly presented by Manuel Clemens in his Romance studies [5]. We follow some stages of his reflections. Let us start, then, in the Enlightenment, the period that grants man freedom of choice, but also requires him to take responsibility for his destiny and thus the moral direction of his actions. In order to clearly define moral direction, Kant formulated the well-known code, the categorical imperative: "Act only according to that maxim by which you can at the same time will that it become a general law." All intelligent beings, and thus all human beings, should examine their actions to see whether they follow a maxim that applies to all, at all times and without exception, and whether in doing so the right of all human beings concerned is taken into account.

Kant does not want one to arbitrarily weigh up what the good could be according to the respective individual case, but postulates that one must always proceed according to the same scheme: If I find myself in a situation that requires a decision to act in a good way, I must necessarily always act in such a way that this action is not only good in this individual case, but would also still be good if all people acted in this way, and could thus be the basis for a generally binding law. Personal needs, desires, and urges are to be sacrificed to the interest of the general public. We are to internalize and apply this code a priori, that is, a priori, independently of all experience, without taking personal interests into account and without responding to the particularity of each situation. Kant thus wants to avoid human passions and other subjective factors undermining the principle of adequate moral action.

This means that man must renounce his personal desires and needs and subordinate himself to duty. A difficult undertaking that can hardly be implemented in practice. For who will subject any action to a separate examination that satisfies these strict criteria?

The classical Schiller therefore modified the path to reason somewhat. Although he also stands behind the principles of the Enlightenment and wants to make man act morally right, he does not believe that Kant's code is feasible, since man is reluctant to renounce his sensual side and possibly cannot do so. But also the feeling of alienation of the individual by too one-sided use of the rational principle, which does not do justice to the essence of the whole human being, led to a rethinking in the classical period. The harmony between reason and feeling or sensuality had top priority.

So how does Schiller's moral education of the individual work if he wants to circumvent the unpopular trajectory of reason, Kant's postulate? Reason usually does not succeed in suppressing sensuality, since instincts are often more powerful than moral insight. That is why Schiller resorts to a trick designed to take consciousness by surprise: The message, i.e. the commandment of the categorical imperative, is given a cloak, namely the form of the work of art, which appeals to people's senses and is therefore not perceived as coercion or pressure. The message is thus on the trajectory of sensuality. Thus, the morality conveyed is experienced and accepted as pleasurable. The bitter medicine of morality is to be experienced as palatable on the sugar coating of art. Schiller, so to speak, uses sensuality as an instrument to channel it. In the glamour of beauty, the idea of the good is to make man integrate it and live it out as much as his desires and lusts. Schiller develops these ideas in his letters "Über die ästhetische Erziehung des Menschen" the philosophy of which can be summed up in the key statement: "Denn, um es endlich auf einmal herauszusagen, der Mensch spielt nur, wo er in voller Bedeutung des Worts Mensch ist, und er ist nur da ganz Mensch, wo er spielt."[3] [6] The realm of art is free, is a field of experimentation for possible beings of existence. Here it is possible to try out which form of life, which ideology is the right one.

Art thus offers a projection surface, independent of the necessity of life, for the unfolding of ideals that capture the essence of man in its full human dimension (essence of reason and feeling). But play, or more precisely aesthetic play, is also what makes him what Schiller calls "fully human." This means that when he is not playing, he is not fully human, but also falls into the category of beings who merely obey the dictates of necessity – see Nietzsche's animals bound by material necessity [7].

As we know, Schiller's experiment to educate people in this way failed on the whole, even if at times a purification of souls may have occurred. The detour via aesthetics has not made people permanently better or led them to experience themselves as whole. Perhaps there is a kind of elation during play, a moment of the sublime that conveys to one what a person might be like if they allowed both reason and emotion to prevail, if they had the freedom to rise above the weight of the moment, of hardship and uncertainty. But how can the experience of such an experience be continued in everyday life without inner overcoming or pressure or coercion? How can one live up to the guiding principle of the classical ideal in daily life? Does one have this constantly in mind?

The detour via art, aesthetic play, only means a shifting of the problem, but not a solution, because the opposition between art and everyday life – according to Clemens – also wants to be overcome, and so he seeks access to the realm that harbours something like wholeness in the sense of a balance of reason and feeling, in the inner space of the human being, as described by Bergson's concept of duration. This concept enables man to seek out a space that does not require him to overcome. Bergson sees freedom in action in the

---

[3] For, to say it out at once at last, man plays only where he is man in the full meaning of the word, and he is only fully man where he plays

two quasi-simultaneous actions in perception: the action directed towards future movement is indeed subject to the dictates of necessity, which animals also obeyed (see above). The second action, however, the selection of memory, is much less strict than the first, because our past experience is an individual and no longer a general one, because we always have many different memories which can fit in the same way to one and the same present situation [8]. Man can evoke the latent images of his choice; since he has several at his disposal, there is no necessity, no compulsion – combinations, new associations are possible – he can play with them.

This moment of arbitrariness, guided by intuition, is for Bergson the moment of freedom of choice, of scope for imagination and creativity. Duration stands for an intuitive understanding of inner time and is the carrier and force of creative change. Here lies the foundation for creative action characterized by personal responsibility. There will be some examples of this in the following chapter.

Let's go back to AI and autonomous driving again. The traffic rule "do not cross solid lines" is of course easy to implement in an AI system. Accordingly, the vehicle would never overtake while crossing a solid line – it would always and exactly follow the rule and in this way act according to the categorical imperative. Now, however, there are many situations in which human drivers violate this rule. They know the situation, the locality, and they interpret the rule as they see fit – and, for example, they overtake the slowly chugging tractor in defiance of the rule. And there are indeed approaches to make this human behavior usable for AI systems and to emulate it. To do this, it is necessary to understand and model processes that are based on memory, intuition and imagination, in order to create a framework for the sometimes generous interpretation of rules.

8.4   The Libet Experiment

The discussion about the freedom of will of humans was extremely lively fueled by an experiment of the psychologist Benjamin Libet in 1979 [9]. His aim was to measure the time between a conscious decision to act and the neuronal activity associated with the action. To do this, a subject was given the task of moving his right hand at any freely chosen time. The subject was asked to observe a kind of running stopwatch and record the time at which he or she voluntarily decided to move the hand. At the same time, EEG was used to measure the brain current activities of the motor cortex, which can be used to read off the readiness potential for initiating the motor action. Libet found that the measured readiness potential was present well before the conscious decision to move the hand. This means that well before the subject's conscious volitional decision, the activity in the brain had already been initiated. Libet's experiments generated debate in a wide range of disciplines about the freedom of the will. Is it unconscious processes in the brain that make decisions that we only later become aware of? Thus one could conclude on the basis of this experiment that we humans do not have free will and thus even the administration of justice would have to be reconsidered, since we do not act fully consciously and thus responsibly. Libet himself tended to believe that the role of free will is not to initiate an action, rather, after the action has been initiated, the conscious decision can be made to stop it or to allow it. This experiment clearly shows that unconscious processes in our brain play an important role – even in seemingly rationally describable actions. Here, we can certainly build a bridge to Bergson's thoughts on intuition and to the considerations that intuition and emotions play an important role in solving even rational tasks such as the Wason Selection Task.

8.5   Summary

Starting from a thought experiment by Laplace, we have argued that the idea of complete determinism cannot be upheld, but rather that chance plays an important and decisive role in the most diverse areas of life. In artificial systems, the question of the predeterminism of action also arises. Using the example of autonomous vehicles, we have shown that here, too, determinism is untenable, which, however, also raises ethical and moral issues to be discussed. We have seen various approaches to making Kant's categorical imperative liveable for humans, and we have also discussed this in the case of AI systems. We concluded the topic of free will with an experiment that suggests arguing against human free will.

References

1. Höfling (1994) Physik. Band II, Teil 1, Mechanik, Wärme. Ferd. Dümmlers Verlag, Bonn
2. BMVI (ed) (2017) Ethik-Kommission. Automatisiertes und Vernetztes Fahren, Bericht des Bundesministeriums für Verkehr und digitale Infrastruktur
3. Bergson H (1939) Die philosophische Intuition. In: Bergson H (ed) Denken und schöpferisches Werden. Libri, Hamburg

4. Mancuso S (2015) Die Intelligenz der Pflanzen. Kunstmann, München
5. Clemens M (2011) Romanische Studien, Nr. 1 Ästhetische Einsamkeit: Bildung außerhalb des Kanons. De Gruyter, Berlin
6. Schiller F (1986) Über die ästhetische Erziehung des Menschen. Reclam Universal-Bibliothek, Stuttgart
7. Nietzsche F (1951) Vom Nutzen und Nachteil der Historie für das Leben. Reclam, Stuttgart
8. Bergson H (2001) Materie und Gedächtnis. Verlag Felix Meiner, Hamburg, Eine Abhandlung über die Beziehung zwischen Körper und Geist
9. Wikipedia. Libet-Experiment – Wikipedia, Die freie Enzyklopädie, 2018. [Online; Stand 18. Oktober 2018]

9

Remembering: A Creative Act

Abstract Memories are the basis of creative design. Access to them and the possibility of modifying them is the theme and content of Proust's and Nabokov's literature, but also in AI. In humans, the process of remembering is carried out in the neural network of the brain. Learning and remembering, i.e. retrieving what has been learned, are also the subject of neuroscience. Parallels to AI are also shown in this chapter.

Works and concepts of two authors can be assigned to Bergson's model of memory: Proust addresses the process of remembering in his novel cycle "Auf der Suche nach der verlorenen Zeit". The focus is on memories stored in the unconscious, which are awakened by a sensory experience and thus perceived. This process leads to a new perception, which is brought to bear through an artistic realization. Nabokov is less concerned with the process than with the structure of memories in the context of time, which he also does not understand as linear. Rather, it is reflected in patterns that constantly expand and weave links by association, in which consciousness ultimately manifests itself.

Some surprising parallels in neuroscience and AI reflect the authors' respective approaches.

© The Author(s), under exclusive license to Springer Fachmedien Wiesbaden GmbH, part of Springer Nature 2023
U. Barthelmeß, U. Furbach, *A Different Look at Artificial Intelligence*,
https://doi.org/10.1007/978-3-658-38474-6_9

9.1   Proust's Memories as a Process

I'm sitting in the car and driving home, it's evening, there's a lot of traffic, I know the route well, I steer the car almost mechanically – without thinking. Now and then, individual manoeuvres, lane changes and the like, demand my attention, which is called upon at short notice. My thoughts are still on the text I just wrote about Bergson's concept of memory. Can I apply this to myself, incorporate it into my life practice? Do his views pass the reality test? What events in life are there that can illustrate his thoughts about memory, recollection, and free will? Class reunions, for example, have something to offer in this regard.

A few years ago… Who are these old people? At first I don't recognize them at all, they have become misshapen, wrinkled – older, unlike me (hopefully). I try not to let my shock show, to keep my composure, to remain polite. Words are exchanged, voice, posture, certain peculiarities evoke the lost contours, the facial features and body shapes lost in the mists of time gradually resurface in memory. One recognizes oneself again. The biographies are briefly completed, people report on what they did after their studies, talk about family and sometimes financial circumstances, which are documented by cell phone photos, and inquire about the progress of the person they are talking to. All well-intentioned, but also a bit stiff and awkward. The sediments of the years have buried the images of memory that were tied to expectations and hopes: The class clown became an elementary school teacher and not a comedian or cabaret artist, the writer of good essays a German teacher and not, as predicted, a writer, the math genius a sales manager for a computer company, the beauty everyone raved about, well … You put a good face on a bad reality. In conversation, they look for links to the past: "Well, son of a gun, you wouldn't have thought that at our age we would still be… " or "Remember Willi…?" and tapping shoulders. In the course of the evening, with the help of alcohol and by inciting each other, the sediments of time are broken open, memories, old stories are exposed, a common chumminess is re-established that couldn't be greater. The 18/19 year olds celebrate their joyous resurgence. My former bench neighbor chuckles as she tells me how I once made her laugh during a geography lesson: "Grandma" asked where the Masurian Lake District was. I whispered in her (the neighbor's) ear, "In your (that is, grandma's) brain box!" – I wasn't actually that wrong in my assumption… – Anyway, within a few hours our distant "durée" as a student had shone again, albeit in the prism of the present certainty of being able to sit back comfortably, let the film rewind, skipping some scenes in the process, watching some in slow motion instead. My somehow still existing being, which at that time fluctuated between shyness and disrespect, timidity and arrogance, the feeling that no one understands me and that everyone can drop dead, this being flared up again and I winked at it: Agreed, yes we belong together. With the happiness in my luggage of being able to relive such moments, I left the hotel early the next morning before the others showed up. I wanted to leave them in my memory, if possible, where our paths had parted. The others probably felt the same way.

However, now our reunion has entered the updated form of "durée" and is stored there. Another sediment has settled in my memory and will possibly be revived on another occasion. So I dived into the past during my car ride, offered some memories (childhood experiences, travels, encounters ...) to the impulse of my action, that is, a mental movement (writing about Bergson), my free will chose the class reunion. The images of the past were recalled like images of a movie, the "real self" identified with these images and projected them into the present animated by the future (wanting to understand Bergson) and at the same time renewed because of their current task, that is, the images were "remembered". The opera arias that I was listening to at the same time supported my feeling of happiness at the richness of the stories that constitute me, my "durée", which, however different, belong to a single "elan vital". Meanwhile, my mechanical memory has let my hands, feet and eyes steer the car. In writing these lines at this moment, there is in turn a recall of the memory (car ride) to the memory (class reunion) in which the school days were remembered.

It is easy to see that, structurally speaking, we are dealing here with a "mise en abyme". The term is used, among other things, for narrative procedures that correspond to mathematical recursion. A well-known textual example is the nursery rhyme:

A dog came in the kitchen and stole a crust of bread.
Then cook up with a ladle and beat him till he was dead.
Then all the dogs came running and dug the dog a tomb
and wrote upon the tombstone for the eyes of dogs to come.
A dog came in the kitchen and stole a crust of bread.
Then cook up with a ladle and beat him till he was dead.

The term "mise en abyme", however, is not to be limited to exactly mirror-image productions; it also covers variations in quantitative, qualitative and functional terms. This structure adheres to many narrative works that also address the narrative procedure as such, and we will encounter it a few more times in our examination of literary works.

Back to the variations of the experience in the process of creation. They are subject to certain "conditions of production" that are related to unconscious memory. For Bergson, it is the action itself that basically blocks or filters the unconscious memory, which is virtually available, and shapes or creatively implements it according to certain criteria with the help of intuition. The criteria are: Suitability of the memory material to support the action, experience in selecting appropriate memories, practice in handling the process of selection. Only when we dream the unconscious has freer rein and can become active relatively unhindered.

When Freud deals with the unconscious, it is not a question of aesthetics that drives him, but the search for a therapeutic way to help a person who shows pathological symptoms that can be traced back to repressed experiences to reconstruct his ego.

Freud draws on Bergson's concept of the unconscious, but modifies it according to the therapeutic objective. His model is based on the idea of the repression of unpleasant memory contents (experiences, conflicts), which are latently present but are warded off by consciousness. They find a way through dreams, among other things, whose unravelling is done through certain interpretative procedures, often with the help of a psychotherapist. In this procedure, a manifest dream content is elicited, which has found an access to the consciousness. In this way, unfulfilled desires, unexpressed situations are compensated and channeled.

Both concepts have in common that they distrust the mind on the surface of consciousness, in their eyes the process of creation occurs at an interface between the unconscious and the conscious. However, they differ in that for Bergson the unconscious is virtually present and retrievable as needed, whereas Freud takes into account the dynamics of psychic forces that block repressed unconscious content for reasons of health (survival despite harmful and hurtful experiences, unpleasant memories, forbidden desires, etc.). Current neuroscientific research supports Freud's concept, which has also been reflected in painting in particular (see Chap. 7).

Here we are interested in the role that the process of remembering can play in the writing of literary works. Proust's novel cycle "Auf der Suche nach der verlorenen Zeit" [1] suggests some parallels with Bergson's model of memory, even though Proust has always resisted referring to Bergson.[1] It is – as Antoine Compagnon conclusively points out in his lecture – not only a work that has memory as its theme, but that is itself constructed like a memory. First, let us briefly discuss Marcel Proust's unusual life, traces of which are reflected in the work, but this should not lead us to confuse the author with the first-person narrator.

---

[1] In the following, we refer, among other things, to the lecture given by Antoine Compagnon at the Collège de France in 2006, entitled "Proust, La mémoire de la littérature".

Marcel Proust was born on July 10, 1871

in the Parisian suburb of Auteuil. His father is a respected doctor and professor of medicine who, in addition to his medical work, devotes himself to brain research and particularly enjoys discussing the function of memory processes with his sons; his mother comes from a wealthy Jewish banking family. As a schoolboy Marcel was already involved in theatre, reading and writing, the most important activities of his later life. After a voluntary year in the military – despite his unstable health, for he has suffered from asthma since childhood – he studies law at the Sorbonne and diplomacy at the École des Sciences Politiques in Paris, but drops out and graduates in philosophy and literature. Under pressure from his father, he took an unpaid job as a librarian in 1895, but soon took a medical leave of absence. It was during this time that Proust met Henri Bergson, to whom he was distantly related.

He leads the life of an idle bon vivant, studies art history and gains access to the bourgeois-aristocratic salon culture, but also to the cream of the princely families (Prince of Wales or the Bavarian King Ludwig). The young dandy observed their customs with meticulous precision and recorded them in his notebooks. Throughout his life, the author struggled with his homosexuality, which his father had tried to exorcise in his youth by sending him to a brothel. Proust had numerous lovers, but never openly admitted his sexual orientation.

The death of his father (1903) and that of his mother (1905), whom he loves idolatrously, trigger a severe depression in him. He tries to fight the inner emptiness left by the loss of his beloved parents with the help of his memory: he sets out in search of the lost time. He withdraws more and more from the glamorous social scene and writes his life's work in bed, surrounded by countless notebooks and pieces of paper. His bedroom is lined with cork oak, because his asthma makes him highly sensitive to noise and smell. That's why he prefers to go out at night – he stimulates himself with mocha – and sleep during the day with the help of Veronal.

In 1913 he published "Du côté de chez Swann", the first volume of his seven-part novel under the main title "À la recherche du temps perdu" (1913–1927), which he concluded with "Le Temps retrouvé" ((The last three parts of À la recherche were published posthumously). The seven books are considered his main work, which has autobiographical features and deals with the nature of human identity. The first volume was already a success. For the following volume he received the Goncourt Prize in 1917. On November 18, 1922, he died of pneumonia in Paris. The last three volumes of his major work are published posthumously.

The novel cycle is preceded by the study "Contre Sainte-Beuve" [2], in which Proust undertakes an intensive poetological reflection on the process of writing and the characteristics of the writing subject, which is later reflected in his epic about memory. In it, he engages with, among other things, the work of the English art critic John Ruskin, which deals with the nature of reading and its effect on the reader. In this treatise, Proust opposes an identification of the biographical and literary self of the writer. The laboratory of the writing subject, he argues, is his "moi profond" as opposed to the "moi social." The proximity to Bergson's distinction of the "moi intérieur" from the "moi conventionnel" is hard to deny! Proust rejects a purely biographical interpretation of poetry. Author and work are, in his view, two independent entities, with the latter as an inner self not so much representing the author as leading the reader to his or her own inner self. Reading, he argues, is an act of communication in the midst of solitude. Accordingly, the real key to truth and knowledge lies not in a book, but in each individual who reads such a book.

The novel has no plot in the true sense of the word, all reality is filtered through the subjective perception of the first-person narrator. It is a novel about time, forgetting and remembering. The narrator discovers by chance that in special moments, with the help of sensual perceptions, past experiences and feelings are uncovered that mean the greatest happiness to him. Despite the length (4000 pages) and the span of the sentences, which can demand some effort from readers, it happens again and again that one falls for him and becomes addicted after bathing in the sea of memories, perhaps because one involuntarily (we will come back to this term more often in a moment) begins to write his book oneself, to communicate in solitude …Let's dive in: "Longtemps, je me suis couché de bonne heure." (For a long time I went to bed early.) So begins the narrator's narrating self, suffering from insomnia, who awakens memories of his earlier bedrooms and ends up in the bedroom of his childhood in Combray. This kind of memory he calls "souvenirs volontaires," memories of the mind, deliberate or arbitrary memories. The narrator ego recalls various phases of his hero's (ego's) life. At a later stage, with the famous madeleine experience, the adult hero will have his first experience of "mémoire involontaire", involuntary memory, which releases a vortex of further memories.

In the Madeleine episode [3], Proust makes the reader witness the individual stages of the act of remembering, which is meticulously structured like a scientific experiment, and makes him sympathize, so that he ultimately believes he is himself digging up the treasure, overcoming obstacles and difficulties, but also feeling the invigorating and exhilarating effect of its recovery. At the beginning of the episode, the narrator reflects on his memories of Combray, long reduced to the drama of going to bed. But then he remembers how, on a winter's day, frozen through and in a depressed mood, he is served a cup of lime blossom tea with a madeleine, a shell-shaped sand biscuit:

When he feels the biscuit softened in the tea in his mouth, he is seized by a feeling of happiness that makes his oppression suddenly give way. To find out the reason for this feeling, he repeats the process, but without success. He realizes that the cause must lie not in the pastry, but in himself. So with the help of his mind he tries to find out what the taste has awakened in him. In order to conjure up the condition once again, he shuts his mind off from all perceptions and focuses entirely on the experience. When this proves fruitless, he offers his mind a kind of relaxation by letting it think of something else. He then makes a second attempt by focusing his concentration on the taste experience again. That's when he feels a stirring awaken within him that he can't yet place. He suspects that it is the visual memory that belongs to this taste. He literally struggles to let this stirring, which keeps wanting to submerge, rise to the surface of consciousness. When he is about to give up, the memory stands before him. The taste was that of that madeleine which his aunt Léonie had offered him at Combray on Sunday morning. It was not the shape of the pastry but its taste that had brought back the memory.

The narrator's other experiences with involuntary memories are also subject to a process of elaboration similar to that described above. Sensory stimuli such as tripping over uneven paving stones or the smell of gasoline from an automobile trigger involuntary memory processes. They act as catalysts for releasing memories related to the original one; they act like a stone thrown into water, leaving many rings on the surface. Thanks to them, from the depths of memory, the past can be brought to light.

The remembered experience is – according to the narrator – more valuable than the past or present, since reality, at the moment it is experienced, cannot employ the imagination, the only organ that can enjoy beauty, since one can only imagine something that is absent [4].

It is through remembering that man becomes an artist, as is revealed in the last volume, "Le temps retrouvé" (Time recovered) [4]. The narrator, who has wanted to become a writer since childhood, reads a passage from the "Journal des Goncourt" (in reality a parody of Proust on the style of the Goncourt brothers) and decides to distance himself from his career aspiration, because if this orgy of description overloaded with adjectives, the soulless copying of reality is supposed to be literature – then he does not believe in his talent. On his way to a reception hosted by the Princess of Guermantes (an old acquaintance of the hero), he ruminates on his supposed flaw of not being able to write. Waiting in a reading room for a piece of music to end, he hears the clatter of a spoon and the rustle of a napkin. These sounds trigger a feeling in him that he once felt on many occasions. This time he decides to deepen his impression, to find out why some sensations make him so happy, and finally understands that involuntary memory alone is capable of reviving the past, and that the work of art allows one to live a real life and overcome the limits set by time. The hero is finally ready to create a literary work. Is the result of this decision, then, the novel we hold in our hands? Are we dealing here with a mise en abyme? It goes without saying that the novel the narrator wants to write cannot be identical to Proust's work. But he evokes a corresponding illusion that allows the narrator's baton to slide, as if casually, into the reader's hand:

In Wirklichkeit ist jeder Leser, wenn er liest, ein Leser nur seiner selbst. Das Werk des Schriftstellers ist dabei lediglich eine Art von optischem Instrument, das der Autor dem Leser reicht, damit er erkennen möge, was er in sich selbst vielleicht sonst nicht hätte erschauen können [4].[2] This inclusion of the reader, indeed the idea that the reader reads himself, is in line with observations about art recipients who, when looking at a painting, undergo creative processes similar to those of the artist (see Chap. 7).

It is possible that the attempt at memory I described at the beginning is influenced by my reading of Proust. How much it has contributed to my perception, I cannot judge for reasons of bias. I can only try out whether I too have memories that are evoked by involuntary experiences. Visiting a place not seen for a long time can trigger involuntary memories of the time and experiences one had in that place: The musty smell of the canal water in Venice, for example, its sloshing against the bank fortifications, the slight vertigo created by the swaying vaporetto stations, the screeching of the seagulls – all of these promote the revival of my Venice feeling, of the memories of this city that I was privileged to visit in my childhood. Or: When I get out of the car after a long drive to the Allgäu, the smell of wood fire brings back my many long winter months. Everyone can test for themselves whether and how sensory stimuli promote memory processes. A part of the lived life that rests in one is reanimated, a note in the keyboard of the ego is struck and lets one of many phases of existence sound. Such moments can be perceived as joyful, they testify to our durée and reveal that the past rests within us and can be recalled. We do not immediately become an artist (unless we capture the experience in a lasting work), but we can read our lives.

We have addressed above all the memories that are more likely to belong to the category of involuntary. Proustian memory experiences are left to pure chance and cannot be brought about willingly. The memories I have described – class reunions, travel experiences – do not actually belong to this category, since I have consciously evoked them in order to illustrate the connection between sensory stimulation and memory. This does not, of course,

---

[2] In reality, every reader, when he reads, is a reader only of himself. In this, the writer's work is merely a kind of optical instrument which the writer hands to the reader so that he may see what he might not otherwise have been able to see in himself.

exclude involuntary recollections, which – of course – tend to be of a rare nature. Proust made use of them as catalysts for a process of remembering, which triggered an avalanche of memories and determined the meshwork of his work, which has the process of remembering itself as its theme.

9.2   Remembering in Neural Networks

Let us look at the processes of learning and remembering from a neuroscientific point of view: We discussed neural networks and, in particular, learning in such networks in detail in Chap. 5. We have seen that learning and storing of knowledge happens by strengthening or weakening connections between neurons. If a connection is used frequently, it is strengthened, and thus the network structure is changed – the network has learned something. In Chap. 7 we then described how such artificial neural networks can be used extremely successfully for image and object recognition. So far, we have said little about retrieving the information that has been stored in the network. We have explained how a network that has learned to classify, for example, to recognize whether an image represents a rose, pushes the pixels through the network with the learned modified connections; at the output of the network there is then a zero or a one, depending on whether it was a rose.

But the detailed Proustian account of the process of remembering from the previous section describes a different problem: how can a memory be made alive? How can the feeling of happiness that triggered the sensation of the madeleine be recreated? How can the Sunday morning in Combray be felt again? In the case of our simple rose example from Chap. 5, this would mean: How can the image of a rose be remembered in the brain without corresponding pixels being applied to the input neurons of the network – i.e. the cells of the retina?

Another peculiarity that we have not yet considered in our artificial neural networks is that human memory consists of numerous different memory systems. We can distinguish between implicit and explicit memory: We learn knowledge about the world, about places and things, i.e. explicit knowledge, which we can make conscious in ourselves when needed; it can then be used and also communicated in the form of language and writing. Implicit knowledge, on the other hand, comprises motor skills, sometimes called procedural knowledge. For example, it is extremely difficult and tedious to learn a good serve in tennis – an explicit or declarative representation, as found in books, does not help much; the movement sequence must be repeated and corrected many times. Only then will the body "remember" and be able to repeat the perfect serve. In connection with Henri Bergson's treatment of time and remembering from Chap. 4, we had spoken of procedural memory; the implicit knowledge is available through a sequence of events, a procedure.

Another dimension is provided by the distinction between short-term and long-term memory: only a very limited amount of information can be stored in short-term memory. For example, when memorizing lists of words, a rough guideline is that up to seven words can be easily remembered and recalled over a short period of time. The exact number varies and is determined by the length of the words presented and by their thematic or semantic context. Without repeated mental repetition of the recorded list, recall is lost after about 18 seconds. Through practice and repetition, however, the information passes into long-term memory and can then be remembered even after a very long time – just as described by Proust. In individual cases, this can also happen without repetition, for example if what is to be remembered is highly relevant. Before we discuss the process of remembering, let us take a closer look at the transition of information from short-term to long-term memory.

Eric Kandel, whom we introduced in detail in Chap. 7, investigated learning and memory on a cellular basis in the 1960s. He used the marine snail Alypsia as a study object, which is distinguished by its small number of cells in the so-called abdominal ganglion – a cell cluster consisting of about 2000 cells. Kandel and his colleagues investigated the gill retraction mechanism: when a certain region near the gill is touched, the snail retracts the gill to protect it. The researchers found that there are two types of learning involved in this simple reflex – habituation and sensitization. In habituation, the Alypsia learns with repeated stimulation that the touch is harmless and weakens the reflex. Sensitization is caused when a painful stimulus is elicited in another region of the body, followed by the non-painful gill withdrawal stimulus. However, as a result of the unpleasant stimulus before it, a violent gill retraction is now triggered. Both forms of learning, however, lead only to a memory in short-term memory. If the stimulus is repeated forty times in succession, a habituation occurs that lasts for one day. Ten stimuli over several days, however, will cause the habit to last up to 4 weeks. The pauses between stimuli apparently facilitate the transition of habituation into long-term memory. Habituation is achieved by suppressing the synaptic connections between the cells of the neuronal system. Sensitization, on the other hand, is achieved by a strengthening of the connections, just as we went through in our small examples with artificial neuronal sections in Chap. 5.

But how does the transition from short- to long-term memory occur? Due to the relatively simple and easily measurable cell structure of the Aplysia, Kandel soon recognized that it is not different regions in which short- and long-term memory are located. They are the same cells in which short- or long-term memory is stored. However, distinct structural changes can be seen in long-term habituation and long-term sensitization. The branching of the neurons increases during sensitization, whereas a loss of synapses can be observed during habituation.

Kandel describes impressively in [5] how years later, from 1980, not least due to the successes of molecular biology, he came to the view that the permanent changes in neurons, i.e. long-term memory, are due to the control of genes in the nucleus of the neurons. A single stimulus – such as touching the gill environment of Aplysia – leads to a strengthening of synaptic connections between neurons. In the case of the gill withdrawal reflex, this is the connection from a sensory to a motor neuron, which is strengthened during sensitization and weakened during habituation. Repeated stimulation causes additional certain enzymes to move into the nucleus. There they activate genes in the cell that have encoded the protein information responsible for synthesizing the protein to modify the compounds. The corresponding protein is synthesized and can be used to permanently form new compounds. This process is much more complex than is implied here – but the important point is that short- and long-term memory are not spatially separated, and that long-term memory is essentially the result of protein synthesis. Research over the past decades has now identified many of the cellular mechanisms involved in learning or storing information, and it has also been shown that the results obtained over decades using simple cell structures, such as those of Aplysia, can also be applied to complex neuronal structures such as those of humans.

Popular textbooks in neuroscience, such as [6], now contain extremely detailed explanations of learning on a molecular biological basis. The situation is different if we want to learn more precisely about remembering. And this is, after all, exactly the process that Proust describes when his protagonist struggles to feel again the Sunday morning in Combray.

Basically, we can distinguish between two different ways in which memory can be accessed: through recognition and through retrieval. When recognizing an object or an event that was perceived or experienced in the past, it is associated with a current object or event. This process obviously requires a comparison, a process that compares new information with that in memory. It can be quite helpful if the environment, i.e. the sensory input, is similar to that of the learning process during recognition. For the special case of face recognition, humans even have a specialized area in the brain that lets us decide very quickly about the familiarity of a face. In the second type, recall, the thing to be remembered is not physically present, it is, for example, the name of a person or a poem learned by heart – here the memory content must be reproduced immediately.

In both cases, oscillations in the brain's neural network seem to play a key role. We have already discussed how a neuron responds to the adjacent connections to other neurons. Once the sum of incoming stimuli reaches a certain potential, the neuron in turn fires across the synaptic connections in the network. This is now not just a single impulse, rather different impulses are fired in succession at a specific rate. Networked neurons in a particular vicinity of the firing neuron now match each other in clock rate. This causes clusters of neurons to align their clock frequency and oscillate together. Such oscillations can be recorded by electrodes on the skull in the form of a so-called EEG. Analyses of EEGs have long played an important role in medicine; that neuronal oscillation also plays an important role in learning and remembering are findings that have only gained acceptance since the 1990s. At that time, Wolf Singer and colleagues were able to confirm the so-called binding-by-synchrony hypothesis through experiments.[3] This made it clear that different regions in the brain can be connected by synchronizing their oscillation. This makes it possible to connect different properties of an object that are stored in different regions of the brain. For example, looking at a tree, the neurons representing the trunk of the tree will synchronize their oscillation with the neurons representing the branches – both regions oscillate synchronously and are thus connected. But neuronal oscillation is also important in learning and reproducing declarative knowledge, such as word lists. This is clearly illustrated by experiments published in [7]. The authors use the tACS (transcranial alternating current stimulation) technique, where electrical oscillations of a certain frequency can be applied to people via electrodes on the scalp. These oscillations now induce a neuronal oscillation in the regions of the neuronal network located in the neighborhood of the applied electrodes. The subject is presented with lists of words to memorize, and a specific frequency is applied using tACS during learning. The rate of correctly reproduced words improves significantly when the same frequency is applied by tACS during recall. If the frequency is changed during recall or if a tACS is applied only for appearance, the same correctness rate is obtained as for the control group without tACS.

The synchronization of neuronal oscillators is thus apparently a mechanism that can link different parts of the brain together as needed. In this way, different information can be linked in different contexts. In experiments with monkeys at the Max Planck Institute for Biological Cybernetics, it was shown

---

[3] I well remember seeing Wolf Singer appear in the computer room during my programming work as a student at the Max Planck Institute for Psychiatry in Munich. He often had a cat in his arms with wires hanging out of its skull. Cats with implanted electrodes in their brains were the basis for these experiments.

that different brain regions synchronize with each other during the recognition of images. The oscillations in the prefrontal cortex, which is essential for short-term memory, synchronize with the oscillations in the visual cortex, where precisely the visual information is processed. So, in a sense, the brain constructs memory by synchronizing the corresponding areas and associating them with each other. Apparently, therefore, links between different objects, properties and images that constitute an event for us are stored in a distributed manner in the brain; if necessary, the links are then restored by synchronizing the oscillation of the corresponding areas.

Let us recall Proust's descriptions: He is trying to recreate the state he felt when he tasted the madeleine and could all at once relive the happiness of his childhood. He describes how he shuts off all his senses and tries to focus on the taste. He describes how visual memories faintly connect with the taste, how a swirl of colors associates with it, how it all suddenly disappears again – and then suddenly the memory is back. Isn't this describing the process of synchronizing oscillation in different areas of the brain? The memory of Sunday mornings is constructed in memory; this is a process that takes place in time, remembering as a formative process! The research results of neuroscience have naturally been obtained with the help of much simpler and therefore easier to understand experiments. Nevertheless, it is exciting to apply the models and explanations developed with them to examples from our daily experience. For example, if we use the loci method (see Chap. 6) to memorize sequences of numbers or lists of words, it could well be that we are using the binding-by-synchrony mechanism described above when we reconstruct the sequences of numbers or lists of words by mentally running through the spatial memorization points. What is certain is that in doing so we are repeating the process of learning – remembering is a constructive temporal process. In a sense, this process is also something creative; memories are constructed and placed in the context of the present. We come to creativity in more detail below.

9.3   Remembering in Artificial Systems

Learning and remembering in artificial neural networks is attempted in a similar way to the living model. However, if one thinks of classical symbolic AI systems that use the mechanisms of knowledge representation and knowledge processing discussed in Chap. 5, the problem of storage and retrieval seems quite straightforward. After all, one of the great strengths of computers is their ability to store data, information, and knowledge in arbitrary quantities. We associate the keyword "big data" with the immense possibilities of processing data from all areas of life, e.g. from social networks or about our purchasing behaviour, and gaining insights into our behaviour. This has become possible due to the almost unlimited storage capacity of our computers or computer networks.

The problem with using large knowledge bases, however, is not storing but finding those parts of the knowledge that are relevant for solving a particular task. Usually, the time constraints are so strict that the knowledge cannot simply be searched until something relevant is found. Consider the use of the Watson system in the Jeopardy! quiz show, which has been mentioned here several times. Here, the answer to a question must be found in the shortest possible time in order to prevail against human competitors. Knowledge is available in sufficient quantities – but how is the relevant part of it identified so that it can be evaluated to find the answer? In Chap. 12 about language we will see that semantic relations between words can be used for this purpose. For example, we know that the term "axe" is used much more frequently in the context of "wood" than, say, in the context of "stone". This semantic similarity can now be used to deploy knowledge in the context of a question involving an axe. Mastering large knowledge bases to find relevant information is a current area of research in AI; unfortunately, we are still far from understanding how humans accomplish this, or even learning from humans.

Another example from the field of symbolic AI and knowledge processing is so-called case-based reasoning. The assumption here is that reasoning in everyday life is essentially based on past experiences. One remembers cases or situations in which one solved a similar problem; now one tries to adapt the solution of the remembered problem to the new one. We know this approach very well from law, where people often refer to precedents that have already been solved in order to deal with a given case. The challenge in case-based reasoning is finding a suitable similarity measure to compare the cases in the case database with the one presented. But again, the task of finding a suitable case can become quite burdensome if there are a lot of cases in the case database. Again, we would like to learn how people accomplish this so quickly and relatively reliably.

We will see later, when we deal with the subject of consciousness, that attention and awareness play an important role especially in these issues.

9.4   Creativity in AI

We have seen that remembering can be understood as a construction, as a process, and that this also represents a form of creativity. The cognitive scientist Margret Boden is one of the few who has dealt with creativity very early in the development of AI research. She defines creativity as the ability to come up with ideas or artifacts that are new, surprising, and valuable. In her widely cited work "The Creative Mind. Myths and Mechanisms" [8], she distinguishes two types of creativity: P-creativity and H-creativity. P-creativity (P as in psychological) involves creating something that is new and surprising to the person creating it. Regardless of how many times the same thing has been created by others, to the person who is creating it, it is creative. Different with H-creativity (H as in historical), here we assume that no one has formulated this idea before, it is so the first time it appeared in history. Of course, H-creativity plays a prominent role in art or science; here it is important who first had the idea. For the study of creativity, Boden notes, it does not matter whether the idea has already been developed by someone else; here there is no need to distinguish between P- and H-creativity; the underlying mechanisms are the same in both types.

Boden describes some examples of creative people who have gone down in history with their discoveries: from Archimedes to the mathematician Poincaré to Marcel Proust. Also very well documented is the nineteenth century discovery of the chemist Kekulé. At that time, the theory (which Kekulé himself had co-founded) was that organic molecules are formed by linear chains of carbon atoms. This had already been demonstrated for many organic compounds, only for benzene this theory did not seem to be applicable. Experiments showed that benzene is composed of six carbon atoms and six hydrogen atoms. However, these building blocks could not be assembled in the usual linear chain model. Kekulé worked on the problem for many months, and no solution seemed possible. Kekulé himself describes the breakthrough: He was sitting in an armchair in front of an open fire one evening, dozing. In his mind's eye he saw various atoms dancing, long rows of atoms forming chains and dancing snake-like with each other. Suddenly one of these snakes got hold of its tail and the circular shape swirled before Kekulé's inner eye. He woke up in a flash – the idea of the benzene ring was there: the atoms could not be arranged in linear chains, but they could probably be arranged in the shape of a ring! Boden now argues that it could not have been the meandering tongues of fire alone that made him think of a ring. Rather, Kekulé may well have had the mathematical concept of open curves in mind; the question then is how this concept was applied in the context of molecular chains, and moreover, what prompted him to conclude the open curves?

Boden distinguishes between different forms of creativity. Central to this is the concept of "conceptual space"; by this she means a structured way of thinking and creating. This can be a style in painting or poetry, it can be a fashion trend or even a theory of a scientific discipline. Such a conceptual space can now be explored and all sorts of new things discovered or different aspects combined in unusual ways. Or the boundaries of the conceptual space can be changed, transformed or abandoned. Just as Kekulé described it using the example of inorganic chemistry.

If we go back to the description of remembering in human memory, we certainly find parallels. There we had made the synchronization of oscillators in different regions of the brain responsible for the combination of different concepts. Is the combination of different concepts in a creative process not related to the process of remembering? Why should such processes not also be able to take place in artificial systems? In the following Chap. 10 we will examine how humour or wit is created by leaving a certain frame. This is not unlike the conceptual space whose alteration or abandonment gives rise to creativity. But first, let's allow Nabokov to show us how art emerges from memories through metamorphosis.

9.5 Nabokov's Memory Patterns

There are few writers who have relied on their memories and used them creatively to such an extent as Vladimir Nabokov. Nabokov knew Marcel Proust's complete works and appreciated his view of art creation: "Proust ist ein Prisma, dessen einziges Ziel darin besteht, das Geschehene optisch zu brechen und damit im Blick zurück eine Welt wieder zu erschaffen, die, wie auch die Menschen darin, von keiner gesellschaftlichen oder geschichtlichen Bedeutung ist"[4] [9]. That is, it is not the political or moral message that matters, but the world as to be recreated. Nabokov's motivation to remember and to record what he remembers, especially in his autobiography "Erinnerung, sprich" [10] is explained in part by his unusually eventful and moving life.

While Proust withdrew from the outer world and, fixated on one point, that is, his bed, reviewed the inner world, Nabokov, because of his migrant fate, is constantly on the move. Nabokov cannot find a fixed point in the outer world, and therefore strives to preserve his inner world, which has its origins in his childhood and youth.

---

[4] Proust is a prism whose only aim is to optically refract what has happened and thus, looking back, to recreate a world which, like the people in it, is of no social or historical significance."

On 23.4.1899 Vladimir Nabokov

was born in St. Petersburg as the eldest of five children. He grows up in an aristocratic family that offers him a happy childhood and youth. His parents are Western-oriented, hire English- and French-speaking governesses and private tutors, and travel extensively in Europe. Vladimir becomes fascinated with butterflies and literature at an early age. He will passionately pursue both ambitions for the rest of his life. His father, a leading politician of the Constitutional Democrats, has to serve a 3-month prison sentence for anti-czarist activities. Later, when the Bolshevists enter the scene, the family has to flee to England via Yalta, and later to Berlin. The October Revolution catapults the 18-year-old Vladimir from the paradise of his childhood at a stroke and turns the potential heir to a huge fortune into a penniless refugee.

Vladimir is studying Russian and French literature at Cambridge. In contrast to many emigrated Russian fellow students, who suffer primarily from the loss of their material resources and privileges, Nabokov is troubled by the fact that the Soviet Russians are destroying his homeland and the hope for humane democratic living conditions in Russia. Vladimir has to cope with another drastic event: In March 1922, his father is killed in the Berlin Philharmonic in a right-wing extremist attack.

A few months later, Nabokov junior moves to Berlin. He writes love poems and stories for the Russian exile community. On the side he works as a tennis and boxing coach and as an extra in the Babelsberg studios. Although Paris becomes more and more important for the Russian emigrants, Nabokov remains in Berlin – and faithful to the Russian language. In 1925 he married the Russian Jewess Vera Slonima, and 9 years later his son Dimitri was born. Nabokov achieved his first successes with the novels "Mary" and "King, Queen, Knave".

In 1937 the family leaves Nazi Germany, lives on the Côte d'Azur, then in Paris. With the novel "The Real Life of Sebastian Knight" (1938), which he had begun there, Nabokov began to write in English, a decision that was not easy for him, but was indispensable for his future as a writer. In 1940 the family moved to the USA, where Nabokov first worked as a butterfly expert at the American Museum of Natural History in New York. As a literature lecturer he teaches at various renowned universities.

Between 1943 and 1951 he writes the first version of his memoirs covering the period from 1899 to 1940 under the title "Conclusive Evidence", (…"conclusive evidence that I really existed…"), in 1967 he publishes the second extended version in America, and in 1984 it is published under the title "Erinnerung, sprich".

In 1955 his novel "Lolita" is published in Paris. It becomes a bestseller and makes its author world-famous and rich at a stroke. Fortunately, his wife saved the scandalous novel about a 37-year-old man's obsession with a 12-year-old girl from destruction – her husband wanted to burn the manuscript!

In 1961 Vladimir and Vera Nabokov move to Montreux, Switzerland, where they occupy a suite in the Palace Hotel. There, in 1969, the novel "Ada oder das Verlangen. Aus den Annalen einer Familie ". In it he combines two initial projects, "Die Textur der Zeit" and "Briefe aus Terra". Nabokov died in Lausanne on 2 July 1977.

Nabokov comments on the source of his creativity in the memoir "Erinnerung, sprich", when he writes of his earliest childhood impressions, which were "…a veritable paradise of visual and tactile impressions."

> Ich erinnere mich, wie ich eines Nachts im Herbst 1903 während einer Reise ins Ausland auf dem (ziemlich flachen) Kissen am Fenster eines Schlafwagens kniete (…) und mit einem unerklärlichen stechenden Schmerz eine Handvoll sagenhafter Lichter sah, die mir von den Falten eines entfernten Hügels her zuwinkten und dann in einer Tasche von schwarzem Samt verschwanden: Diamanten, die ich später an meine Figuren verschenkte, um die Bürde meines Reichtums zu erleichtern. Wahrscheinlich hatte ich das festsitzende geprägte Rouleau am Kopfen de meines Bettes losgemacht, und meine Fersen waren kalt und ich spähte weiter."[5]

These impressions belonged to the harmonious world of a perfect childhood [10].

The diamonds he has to give away, for example, are crayons, which Nabokov conjures up and puts into action to visualize little Vladimir's desire to paint and his imagination suitably set in motion. These pencils were distributed to fictional children in his books to keep them occupied, a loss the poet regrets! He feels the passing on of a personal memory to the sphere of art as a kind of dispossession: He had the impression that valuable components of his past, with which he endowed his novel characters, withered away in fiction, lost their personal connection, and belonged more to the novel than to his self. For Nabokov, the creative transposition of an experience always means a kind of alienation of the experience that devalues or revalues its original meaning.

Nabokov acknowledges that historical and genetic factors are part of the memoirist's craft, but resists seeing in them "[…] with certainty the tool that shaped me, that anonymous roller that imprinted on my life a certain artistic watermark, whose unique pattern comes to light when the writing paper of life is shone through with the lamp of art." As an artist, Nabokov wants to make visible the patterns of individual mystery. How these come about, what significance they have for his existence and worldview, Nabokov describes in the following words, which are quite compatible with the observations of Bergson and Proust: "Ich gestehe, ich glaube nicht an die Zeit. Es macht mir

---

[5] I remember kneeling on the (rather flat) cushion at the window of a sleeping-car one night in the autumn of 1903, during a trip abroad (…) and seeing, with an inexplicable stabbing pain, a handful of fabulous lights waving at me from the folds of a distant hill and then disappearing into a pocket of black velvet: Diamonds that I later gave away to my characters to lighten the burden of my wealth. I had probably unfastened the stuck embossed rouleau at the head of my bed, and my heels were cold, and I peered on.

Vergnügen, meinen Zauberteppich nach dem Gebrauch so zusammenzule-gen, daß ein Teil des Musters über den anderen zu liegen kommt. [...] Und am meisten genieße ich die Zeitlosigkeit, wenn ich [...] unter seltenen Schmetterlingen und ihren Futterpflanzen stehe. Das ist Ekstase, und hinter der Ekstase ist etwas anderes, schwer Erklärbares. Es ist wie ein kurzes Vakuum, in das alles strömt, was ich liebe. Ein Gefühl der Einheit mit Sonne und Stein. Ein Schauer der Dankbarkeit, wem sie auch zu gelten hat – dem kontrapunk-tischen Genius menschlichen Schicksals oder den freundlichen Geistern, die einem glücklichen Sterblichen zu Willen sind."[6]

Nabokov also discovers a kind of magic in the mimicry of butterflies, whose distinctiveness goes far beyond what nature or its actual purpose demands. The imitated appearance and behaviour could not be explained by natural selection in the Darwinian sense, the theory of the struggle for existence was insufficient when the predator is overtaxed with the subtle protective measure taken with great effort. In literature, too, the magical has a high value. A good writer, according to Nabokov, is above all a magician! [9]

Even though Nabokov draws heavily on his social background and per-sonal and contemporary historical experiences, especially in his biography – for understandable reasons – he sees artistic creation as an expression of "purposeless delight", which he also finds in nature. He is far removed from a reduction of life and especially of art to deterministic factors. For Nabokov, the source of creativity is memory; he constructs memory anew each time. Time plays a role, but it is constantly distorted and changed. Much as we observed in Proust and described in the neuroscientific description of mem-ory: Remembering as a creative and creative process!

Another non-biographical work, "Ada oder das Verlangen",[7] is recursive like Proust's cycle of novels, that is, at the end of the novel we find ourselves at the beginning of its writing, namely the memoirs of the protagonist Van, commented on by his lover Ada. "Ada" is the story of the incestuous love between siblings Van and Ada, who first meet at the Ardis family estate and then meet again after 4 years, with already hints of jealousy causing tension. For decades, the two will try to avoid each other, search for each other, meet each other, and ultimately find each other again – at the age of about Fifty – to

---

[6] I confess, I don't believe in time. It gives me pleasure to fold my magic carpet after use so that one part of the pattern comes to lie over the other. [...] And I enjoy timelessness most when I stand [...] among rare butterflies and their food plants. This is ecstasy, and behind the ecstasy is something else, hard to explain. It's like a brief vacuum into which everything I love flows. A feeling of oneness with the sun and stone. A frisson of gratitude to whomever it may be – the contrapuntal genius of human fate, or the kindly spirits at the will of a fortunate mortal.

[7] Ada or Ardor: A Family Chronicle.

reunite and have a relationship that lasts more than 40 years. The ninety-year-old Van writes the "Family Chronicle", a complex demonstration of his theory about the nature of time. This is explained in the form of a lecture on "The Texture of Time" which Van transcribes as a lecturer in psychology and philosophy. It essentially states that time is not linear and runs in one direction, but that it is erratic and can also run backwards. – Significantly, there are also ironically dressed up references to Bergson and Proust in this treatise. – The "arrow of time" as a symbol of linear time undergoes a blatant inversion as Van, the 90-something, vividly evokes youth far in the past in precise detail. The reader experiences the erotic advances of the youth with their expectations of what is yet to come, that is, the "not yet", and at the same time senses the whiff of the "no more" that the mature couple exudes. It is not a retrospective, then, but a present consciousness informed by the past. Van specifies this by pointing out that present is only an "imaginary point", yet that what we are conscious of as present is a constant building up of the past, of its smooth and ceaselessly rising level. Bergson sends his regards!

At the novel's intersection, when Van is transcribing the lecture on "The Texture of Time", that is, questioning the linearity of time, he is on a trip to Switzerland to meet Ada again, whom he has not seen in 17 years. When she answers the phone at the hotel, he euphorically perceives her telephone voice, hitherto unknown to him: The telephone voice that linked past to present formed the centerpiece in his deepest perception of tangible time, the "glittering now" that was the only reality in the texture of time. But, as if to give the lie to his concept of time, he is cruelly confronted with transience: "Nach der Glorie des Gipfels kam der schwierige Abstieg."[8] What follows is a meticulous description of the ravages that time has wreaked on Ada's body. However, the signs of her beloved's age are not hidden from her either. The expected exuberance of reunion gives way to embarrassing self-consciousness. It seems as if transience, the arrow of time, should be proved right; the couple part embarrassed. Ada pretends to have to travel to Geneva, Van anesthetizes himself with a sleeping pill.

The next morning, however, when he realizes that he must act quickly in order not to lose Ada and looks out of the balcony, he sees, engrossed in the view one floor below, how she voluptuously scratched the thigh below the right buttock. The spell is broken when he kisses her hands. He defied death and put the terrible fate to flight.

Van's notes on the lecture begin with a rejection of determinism. A student reminds the lecturer that he is going to die after all, which means that the

---

[8] After the glory of the summit came the difficult descent.

future is a factor of time. Van asks the counter-question: Who said I (high-lighted in the original) was going to die? and explains that past and present are shrouded in unconsciousness. Only a brief span of consciousness, the present, tells him that he has passed through something like the past; the future is at best the idea of a hypothetical present based on our experience of sequence, on our belief in logic and habit. In every moment it is an infinity of branching possibilities. Unsurprisingly, the death is whisked away at the end by a narra-tive trick. Van and Ada's death is not portrayed in the novel; the narrator merely speculates, "Man kann sogar vermuten, dass unser Paar, auf dem Rücken hingestreckte Märtyrer der Dauer [sic], falls es je zu sterben gedachte, sozusagen in das vollendete Buch hineinsterben würde, hinein in Eden oder Hades, in die Prosa des Werks oder die Poesie seines Waschzettels."[9]

The whole plot of the novel is set on "Antiterra". It resembles Earth in many geographical and historical details and offers a luxurious dreamscape of ancient Russia, modern America and antiquated Europe, an artificial para-dise. It is fairy-tale-like and not, as it might seem, science fiction, which the author abhors. Nabokov is concerned with creating a fictional cosmos in which the "texture" of time, i.e. its nature for human consciousness, comes to view. Antiterra, then, is not meant to be particularly different from our world, but only to distract from our world, to free the message from the gravity of reality and make it more accessible.

Brian Boyd, a New Zealand literary scholar who has studied "Ada" exten-sively, discovers in Nabokov's work hints that we do not recognize the pattern of our life as long as we are trapped within human time. The reader should see both the limits of mortal life and the freedoms that may lie beyond it. [12]. In this, Boyd recalls Nabokov's remark (in the latter's work on Gogol) that only a single letter separates the comic from the cosmic, and conjectures that the work "Ada" asks whether there is something playful behind life-not in the sense that reduces life to a meaningless game, but something that makes it so much richer. According to Boyd, Nabokov, who as a butterfly scientist had studied the concepts of genus (idea of sameness) and species (idea of differ-ence) in depth, had created a microcosm with "Ada" that shows how con-sciousness grasps the world, namely through increasing perception of differences and sameness. It is a world of patterns woven together from sounds and words, colors and outlines, things and characters, dates and events, an imitation of our terra.

---

[9] One may even suppose that our pair of supine martyrs of duration [sic], if they ever intended to die, would die, as it were, into the completed book, into Eden or Hades, into the prose of the work or the poetry of its wash-sheet.

Even though they deal differently with the factors of time, memory and creativity, the authors Bergson, Proust and Nabokov share a common approach. Nor is it surprising that Proust knew Bergson's writings and that Nabokov was taken with Bergson and Proust. In the volume "Deutliche Worte" [13],[10] a collection of interviews, essays and letters to the editor, Nabokov expresses his envious admiration for the great storytellers of the century, Proust and Kafka, and at the top James Joyce, the author of "Ulysses", and the philosopher Bergson – to them he feels a kindred spirit. Their creative work is linked to the question of how perception and memory function. The factor of time plays an essential role in this. Like Bergson and Proust, Nabokov rejects the idea that the process of remembering can be reduced to a repetition of the temporal linear sequence of an event. The complexity of the process of remembering, or of conveying what is remembered, is bound up in the act of creating. The author's personality is composed of many components and transcends deterministic factors such as social conditions, hereditary factors, moral and political purpose, being able to create different individual works that defy the cause-effect mechanism. For Nabokov, this moment, freedom from deterministic implications and freedom from missionary aspirations (political or religious), is one of his criteria for the quality of a work of art. Another criterion is the adequate use of language and knowledge of the world: "Der Schriftsteller muß sorgfältig die Werke seiner Rivalen studieren, eingeschlossen die des Allmächtigen. Er muß die angeborene Fähigkeit besitzen, die vorgefundene Welt nicht nur neu zu kombinieren, sondern neu zu erfinden. Um dies angemessen zu tun und keine doppelte Arbeit zu machen, sollte der Künstler die vorgefundene Welt kennen"[11] [13]. The re-creation of the world, then, is not a vague fabrication detached from reality, but requires the instrument of exact perception and pedantically precise representation. In this, too, he agrees with Bergson and Proust. It is left to the reader to find himself in the newly created world and/or to create one for himself.

9.6   Summary

We started from Marcel Proust's description of the memory process in "Auf der Suche nach der verlorenen Zeit". There it became clear that memories are generated by a process. The triggering of this process does not always happen

---

[10] Strong Opinions.

[11] The writer must carefully study the works of his rivals, including those of the Almighty. He must possess the innate ability not only to recombine but to reinvent the found world. In order to do this adequately and not duplicate work, the artist should know the found world.

consciously. The Proustian description coincides surprisingly well with the findings of neuroscience about learning and remembering. In doing so, we have essentially drawn on the work of the neuroscientist Eric Kandel and some more recent aspects about the synchronization of oscillators in the brain. We compared this learning and remembering in neural networks with the storage and retrieval of information in symbolic AI systems. It became clear that in symbolic systems knowledge is tangible, it can be extracted and further processed. In neural networks, what is learned is present in the form of weights at the connections throughout the network; here it is (currently) still impossible to extract or communicate individual aspects of what is learned.

We have interpreted remembering as a creative process and could therefore also apply Margret Boden's concept of conceptual space to it. Nabokov's past forms a framework, in which he recombines facts, also goes beyond them and reinvents.

References

1. Proust M (1950) Auf der Suche nach der verlorenen Zeit. Suhrkamp, Frankfurt
2. Proust M (1954) Contre Sainte-Beuve. Gallimard, Paris
3. Proust M (1981) Auf der Suche nach der verlorenen Zeit, Bd 1. Suhrkamp, Frankfurt
4. Proust, M (1964) Auf der Suche nach der verlorenen Zeit, Bd 7. Suhrkamp, Frankfurt
5. Kandel E (2006) Auf der Suche nach dem Gedächtnis. Siedler, München
6. Kandel E, Schwartz JH, Jessell TM et al (2000) Principles of neural science, Bd 4. McGraw-Hill, New York
7. Javadi A-H et al (2017) Oscillatory reinstatement enhances declarative memory. J Neurosci 37(4):9939–9944
8. Boden MA (2004) The creative mind. Myths and mechanisms. Routledge, London
9. Nabokov V (2014) Vorlesungen über westeuropäische Literatur. Rowohlt, Hamburg
10. Nabokov V (1991) Erinnerung, sprich. Rowohlt, Hamburg
11. Nabokov V (2010) Ada oder das Verlangen. Eine Familienchronik. Rowohlt, Hamburg
12. Boyd B (2005) Vladimir Nabokov. Die amerikanischen Jahre 1940–1977. Rowohlt, Hamburg
13. Nabokov V (1973) Deutliche Worte. Rowohlt, Hamburg

10

Frame and Structure

Abstract Memorized contents are experienced emotionally differently. Why is it that something exhilarates us, frightens us, unsettles us? The factors that influence us obey the dictates of being alive and are regulated by conventions. In order to enable orientation between knowledge bases, AI uses corresponding delimited areas or frames.

We are at the circus: two clowns are presenting their act. They stumble clumsily around the ring, bump into each other, fall down, get up again, kick each other, press cakes into each other's faces, and so on. The audience reacts in different ways: the adults smile with effort, older children shriek with delight, smaller ones press themselves crying against their parents, the performance frightens them.

A party among teenagers: bored mood. We, a friend and I, look out the window, follow the traffic and start laughing at the cars. How they secretly follow each other, give each other signs, communicate with each other! An inexhaustible spectacle with multiple variations. We laugh our heads off, while the others think we are not "all there", have even "taken something". Not true at all, we have simply found a code that imputes some kind of will or intention to the mechanical devices. Those who don't know this don't find it funny, feel locked out.

An exhibition of works by Jean Tinguely in Munich: The artist has recreated an altar scene. Praying figures performing the rituals in the church, crucifying themselves, bowing, kneeling, folding their hands, etc., can be set into action at the push of a button. One visitor shakes his head in pique at this supposed blasphemy. When I happen to glance in his direction again, I see him – imagining himself alone – operating the button, smiling.

© The Author(s), under exclusive license to Springer Fachmedien Wiesbaden GmbH, part of Springer Nature 2023

U. Barthelmeß, U. Furbach, *A Different Look at Artificial Intelligence*,
https://doi.org/10.1007/978-3-658-38474-6_10

Our consciousness is constantly in motion, it must be able to assess situations, weigh up behaviors, evaluate, react skillfully, be resourceful, have presence of mind. At the same time, however, it also requires a certain routine through repeated practice and learned procedures that one uses more or less unconsciously to master everyday life (see procedural memory). It is not always easy to balance the use of both attitudes appropriately, to stay within the bounds of what seems reasonable and adequate, which can lead to a disturbing imbalance.

If there is such a disproportion, if there is a disturbance with regard to the "frame" – we will discuss this term in more detail – emotional reactions such as cheerfulness, fear, horror, irritation, etc. occur, which can also be mixed. How does this work? What serves as our guide for the appropriate use of the two tendencies, i.e., the alert and the routine response? What does frame mean?

Bergson's remarks on laughter [1] give us valuable clues to the framework as far as the realm of the comic is concerned. The French humanities scholar Jean Luc Giribone discovers parallels to the uncanny in Sigmund Freud and brings both theoretical approaches together in his work on the comic and the uncanny [2]. In doing so, he recognizes that both domains, that of the comic and that of the uncanny, belong to the same category. This is also supported by psychoanalytic research, namely by means of Marguerite-Albert Séchehaye's "Journal d'une schizophréne de la psychanalyste". He succeeds in transferring the concept of frame to other areas of life and thus provides explanatory approaches as to how our behaviours and emotional reactions are possibly controlled.

First of all, Bergson. Laughter, or the comic, is ideally suited for him to explain the main features of his life-oriented philosophy. He sees in laughter something alive, conducive to life, and the comic as something that is in its own way reasonable and, like the dream, "methodical in its irregularity" and can provide information about the human imagination, its workings in life and art [1]. He does not search for the formula of the comic, but observes how comedy arises or is produced, examines whether its production process can be transferred to similar cases, and thus arrives at an overall view of the comic.

He places three fundamental observations at the beginning, namely, firstly, that comedy occurs only in the realm of the human,[1] since nature as such is not funny (the animal only when human features are placed under it); secondly, that it presupposes insensibility, i.e., a certain mental coldness, if not pure intellect, for pity or love prevent the necessary distance from the action,

---

[1] Bergson could not have known the approach of artificial intelligence at that time.

and thirdly, that this intellect communicates with other intellects, that is, that laughter presupposes a sense of community with other laughers (real or imagined). The latter is an indicator of the social function of laughter as a correction of misbehaviour.

Bergson's parade example: a man is walking in the street, trips over a stone, falls to the ground, the passers-by laugh. They wouldn't do it if they knew he sat down on purpose. They laugh because he did it involuntarily, because he was clumsy and didn't change his course. They laugh at his lack of agility, absent-mindedness, lack of adaptability, that is, at the fact that, according to the law of inertia, the muscles continued their motive activity. Surely Bergson had some kind of slapstick scene in mind, because it is not necessarily exhilarating when someone falls down. I'm thinking of the butler in the sketch "Dinner for One," he's drunk and trips over the skull of a lion-skin rug. His waking consciousness paralyzed, he stubbornly walks straight ahead, oblivious to the pitfalls of his path. The spectator laughs at his misbehavior. The butler does not learn as he stumbles again and again. The spectator continues to laugh, but eventually becomes accustomed to the drunk's behavior, until the same stops completely unexpectedly (and even more drunk than before!) in front of the lion's head and hops over it. Now the audience roars, for it has found itself becoming lethargic, having fallen asleep and allowed the movement to become routine. It basically laughs at its misjudgement regarding the candidate (this one was capable of learning after all!) and ultimately at itself.

This scenery can be applied to many slapstick acts. Wherever rigidity and immobility occur, comedy ensues: people with a fixed idea, such as Don Quixote who thinks he is a knight, constantly fall on their faces and get a beating; life trips them up and they are therefore subject to ridicule. Deficiencies of character, a form of paralysis of the soul, such as rigid insistence on certain principles, have always been the subject of comedies. Molière's "miser" Harpagon, who has become rich but remained stingy and narrow-minded, almost ruins the future of his children, who want to enjoy life, thus acts against "bon sens," common sense, and is laughed at. Orgon falls for a sanctimonious hypocrite named Tartuffe, who turns him into a puppet and makes him put Tartuffe's welfare above that of his family. When his wife literally shows him how Tartuffe is deceiving him – Orgon witnesses the lecherous Tartuffe getting into his wife's pants – it is almost too late.

Let's think of the successful US sitcom "The Big Bang Theory", which is about highly intelligent young physicists whose shared flat opposite the apartment of the pretty waitress Penny. The two nerds and computer geeks are constantly getting into trouble due to their naivety and social incompetence; their lack of flexibility, as well as the resulting automatism of their behavior, contrasts with the common sense of their alert neighbor. The laughter element is their automatism, their lack of competence to communicate meaningfully in their everyday environment.

Life demands incessant adaption; he who resists and reveals rigidity of character, mind, and body is ridiculed: "This rigidity is the comic, and laughter is its corrective."

Bergson uses many other examples to illustrate his famous formula: "Le comique, c'est du mécanique plaqué sur du vivant", i.e. "The comic is the mechanical superimposed on the living" or "The comic is the mechanical incrusted on the living". Mechanical manifests itself in repetition: a speaker makes a certain gesture that is not funny in itself; however, when the gesture recurs as a tick and one gets the impression that it is repeated regardless of the speaker's will, the situation becomes comic. Repetition and imitation seem comical because "[...] life should not repeat itself." Repetition is a precursor of rigidity, of the lifeless, material. Materiality is therefore the hallmark of the comic and is banished from the tragic: A speaker who sneezes seems ridiculous – the spiritual is disturbed by the physical. In tragedy, activities such as eating, drinking, or the satisfaction of other human needs are taboo; they remind us that man is (also) matter, distract us from conflicts of a spiritual nature, reduce him, to put it exaggeratedly, to a thing. Such a thing is per se, as an extreme form of inertia, the absolute antithesis of the living.

In classifying comic scenes, Bergson identified three primal scenes: the jack-in-the-box, the puppet, and the snowball. These mechanisms are the ancestors of a multitude of other comic arrangements.

The jack-in-the-box jumps out of his box as often as you push him down. The mechanism of the popular children's toy is taken up in many scenes in different forms: The policeman who is knocked down by a blow on the head in Punch and Judy, gets up again, gets another blow, and so on. The chases in the silent films: Charly Chaplin is pursued by policemen, changes direction, and the next squad of hundreds is already coming towards him, etc. or speech duels that take place through a kind of firing off of coordinated replicas, as in Molière's comedies.

The mechanism of the puppet, Bergson's second primal scene, is embodied in persons who believe they are acting freely, but are in fact the playthings of a passion or the victims of a habit. Bergson recounts a true incident: A passenger ship was wrecked near Dieppe. Some passengers managed to escape onto a boat with difficulty. Customs officers bravely came to their aid, but asked them if they had nothing to declare [1]. Duteousness has a firm grip on the brave men. They cannot escape it, even when circumstances make absurd their routine approach. Déformation professionnelle is always a popular theme in comic scenes. Think of Loriot's "Papa ante portas": Heinrich Lohse, a purchasing director at Deutsche Röhren AG who has taken early retirement, acts as a business economist in the household, much to the chagrin of his wife, and wreaks all kinds of havoc in the process.

And finally the snowball, it rolls and rolls and gets fatter as it rolls. A bumped tin soldier triggers the toppling of a row of tin soldiers. One household mishap is chained to others: In the sketch "Das Bild hängt schief"[2], Loriot tries to straighten a picture that is hanging crookedly, but this leads to further disorder in the room (tables tipped over, shelves emptied.). Every effort to counteract the chaos only leads to further mess, until finally the room is totally devastated.

The primal scenes of laughter have their roots in early childhood, and Bergson assumes that when we enjoy ourselves as adults, we bring to mind memories of past feelings experienced in childhood. It is only necessary to examine carefully what of our pleasures are merely memories, and to shorten them down in order to encounter the original feeling [1].

However, these primal scenes, which at first glance seem comical, can also be seen from a completely different perspective. Giribone explores this phenomenon. He takes a hint from Bergson about participants in serious and solemn ceremonies. These would remind us of puppets as soon as we forget the object of the serious solemnity [1]. Giribone [2] turns this idea around: as soon as we forget the comedy of a sketch, the puppets taking part in it can seem to us as if they were taking part in a ceremony, a serious solemnity whose object we do not know. He thus bridges the gap to Sigmund Freud's uncanny, noting that the instrument of repetition can be used to create both a serene and an uncanny mood.

For example, he plays with the idea of repurposing an uncanny experience of Freud's. Freud recounts the following incident: He got into a dubious neighborhood with heavily made-up women at the windows. Repeatedly he tried to leave the area, got lost and ended up in the same street again and again, causing a stir. This seemed uncanny to him and he was relieved when he found his way again [3]. Giribone can imagine a satirical version of this experience: the buttoned-up Viennese scientist, who to the horror of bourgeois moralizers emphasizes the omnipresence of the sexual, feels uncomfortable in the presence of prostitutes, tries to escape them, and repeatedly gets caught up in their swirl.

From the possible congruence of the comic and the uncanny, Giribone concludes that both areas can be assigned to the same region, which is only described differently, seen differently, as if one were the negative photograph of the other.

---

[2] The picture is crooked.

In order to understand this identity and the reversibility of the domains, he uses the concept of frame, exactly as Bergson often does. For example, when we find the resemblance of a real person to a novel character funny, it is not because of the character of the novel, which does not necessarily have to be ridiculous, but it's comical to resemble the character, to fit into a ready-made frame. Of course it is also comical when you yourself congeal into a character, become a frame into which others fit [1]. Bergson gives other vivid examples of frames. Trades and professions, for example, are such: They are causes of habits, ways of speaking, certain behaviors. Bergson speaks of "professional hardening" (the famous "déformation professionnelle") or "professional obduracy". One can also extend this consideration to social classes, epochs, geographical origins, and the like. They are all possible frames, but their peculiarities are not ridiculous as such; they only become so when they give a particular action or situation a frame that is not appropriate to it. The comic, then, is not an intrinsic quality; it is a tool.

Giribone traces the term frame, which Bergson does not further define, and finds it in Gregory Bateson, an anthropologist and learning theorist [4]. His research begins with the observation of two young monkeys playing with each other by miming a fight. The behaviors seemed to resemble those that occur in a real fight charged with aggression, but it was clear to them and to the observer that the fight was really a kind of non-fight. So there was the somehow voiced message: this is a game.

The frame here is a kind of general meta-message that touches all messages and signals that take place within its location. This frame is conceptualized, for example, film, game, interview, work, sometimes there is no verbal reference to the frame and you are not aware of it. Each of these frames determines the value of the elements contained within it.

Frames often form symmetrically occurring pairs of opposites, such as game and seriousness, work and leisure, and so on. They determine the content of what is experienced and can even reverse it: Aggression can become banter, pain pleasure, fear pleasure. How can one watch a horror movie with pleasure? Giribone explains this paradox with the frame that fear is given, namely that of a leisure pleasure. For fear as such does not disappear. The frame of leisure pleasure or holiday activity turns the pain of sport or other strenuous activities into attractive occupations that would otherwise – in the context of work or duty – be perceived as unreasonable torture.

Even if the relationship of the frame to its elements may seem paradoxical in the above examples, it works. The situation is different, however, when the connection between the frame and what is framed is disturbed and is no longer needed in the sense of logic. When the frame moves away from what it is supposed to frame, the connection loosens and a gap is created. The frame becomes independent until it no longer has anything to do with the content. One enters here, according to Giribone, the universe of the fantastic narrative, in which all the elements are related to a frame that is not named, but which in a certain sense superimposes them, and it is precisely through this superimposition that its disturbing presence is manifested: We are in Kafka's universe. In the novel fragment "Der Prozess" [5], the trial itself, with its persecutions, accusations and constraints, does not fit with what is narrated – K., the novel's protagonist, has done nothing that could lead to a trial, the frame is imposed on him, literally falls upon him; this lack of context, the absence of a meaningful connection, this superimposition constitutes the originality and the power of Kafka's universe. Giribone speaks here of a "pathology" of the frame. Whereas in the "trial" the frame is outside the character and descends upon him, in the novel fragment "Das Schloss" it sits inside the character: it is about a person who tries at all costs to get into a castle and no one understands why. The reasons put forward at the beginning, surveys, etc., evaporate and are never really credible; they give way to a frantic search that relies on no psychological moment, on no probability inside the fictional coordinates. The enigma sits within the person – and frames the fiction.

Another impairment of the frame happens when a foreign object embeds itself in the material of the framed. Something that the frame cannot actually encompass penetrates it and pierces it. Giribone recalls a sketch by Raymond Devos on the subject of bread and bakers. When he casually mentions the question of world hunger, the laughter dies down. The comedian comments, "You don't laugh anymore!", lingers briefly on this tragic topic, as if to walk off the boundaries of the comic, and then returns to the interior of the original frame. Something similar happened in a german cabaret: a comedian deals with the situation of guest workers and their relationship with the natives. The laughs die down, however, when, in a vision of the future, he predicts to the audience that they will one day have to emigrate to Australia to work as labourers. A whole category of fantastic stories is based on the emergence of signs that weaken and then finally break the frame of initial probability. You think you're dealing with a narrative, and eventually realize it's a dream, as at the end of Alice in Wonderland. In these cases, the frame is not self-contained; it is related to the narrative material, but is contradicted by elements of that material, possibly becoming distant until it disappears. It is either replaced by another frame (a fantastic one instead of a probable one, for example) or we are left hanging in a frameless region. And this frameless region is that of the uncanny par excellence. If this strangeness is unsettling, it is because a situation presents itself without its instruction manual, without clues as to how it should be understood, without the general whole to which it belongs. The frame is no longer merely fragile, distorted or questioned, because all these operations would more or less imply its continued existence. But if the frame withdraws entirely from the field of vision, the feeling of the uncanny emerges: New elements that gradually emerge break the initial narrative coordinates and make appear an aspect that defies any reassuring logic. On the one hand, one damages the frame whose function was to collect and classify a variety of elements; on the other hand, what appears through the hole is not a different or reconfigured frame, but it is completely outsourced. The "healthy" frame of the comic, on the other hand, even when deformed and stiffened, is preserved as a point of reference; it is present like a yardstick by which to judge excess, madness, or the absurd automatism in a situation. The ridiculous customs officers are super-customs officers , they do too much of a good thing; the ridiculous philosophers of the comedies are too philosophical with their incomprehensible gibberish; the gesture of a speaker, perfectly acceptable in itself, is repeated in excess and becomes comic. We do not enter here into another universe, remain in ours, even if it darkens or deforms, it points indirectly to that from which it departs.

This fundamental difference can also be expressed in terms of the distance of the ego from the frame. In comedy we observe a spectacle that does not include us. The effect of comedy is based on the fact that we do not identify with the situation or the person. The uncanny, on the other hand, pierces the frame, reaches out to the observer, and involves him or her in the spectacle. We wonder with the protagonist, we are speechless with him, troubled, we are afraid with him. This piercing of the frame also attacks our ego. – This is basically not surprising either, because the term frame means almost the same thing in family therapy as the ego does in psychoanalysis. They are two instances of systems.

Giribone finally explores the question of what is in the frame. What does the frame actually frame? He finds the answer in Bergson: it is life – in its unpredictable freedom of unfolding, which, far from our automatisms and our rigidities, realizes its verve and its grace. Language tries to live from this unfolding, but it succeeds only imperfectly: Our language lives from our life. It would elude the comic if it were perfect, if there were no rigidness about it, if it were a unified organism that could not be split. It would then resemble a pond, but there is none whose surface would be free of foliage [1].

Bergson's view is based on a view of life as unfolding par excellence, which is different from anything that attempts to make this conscious, such as language and thought. Thought takes place in the face of the movement of life and is coarse, not detailed, not specific enough in relation to it. Bergson accuses previous philosophers of not being precise enough. Even if the rivers were to flow upward, if there were no plants and animals, if we did not need food, their assertions would remain the same [6].

Our perception of reality is due to the principle of the living. In order to live, the human must extract the impressions of things useful to him and react to them appropriately. The other impressions elude his attention. Our perception of the external world, then, is what our senses filter out of things for us to act upon. We are dealing with a practical simplification of reality, purged of useless features and emphasizing the useful ones. Thus, over time, certain pathways of perception have been formed on which our actions are based. The classification of things obeys the imperative of their usefulness [1]. The human, he says, is certainly superior to the animal in this respect; the wolf would make no difference between a goat and a lamb; we would distinguish a goat from a mutton, but hardly a goat from another goat. That is, the individuality of things escapes us when it is of no practical use to us to notice it. We usually only see the labels stuck on things and this tendency has increased under the influence of language: The word steps between us and the things, it would hide their shape, if it were not already hidden by the restriction of the usefullness. Now and then an artist lifts the veil that is between things and us, frees us from the prejudices that have interposed themselves between our perception and reality. These "souls", meaning the unbiased artists, that is, the artists who are free from prejudice, owe their existence to a kind of "absent-mindedness" (sic!) of nature. That would mean, then, that nature, too, is not always alert, becomes indolent, which helps people to come closer to it. Bergson's view of the frame content, basically of the world, reveals how rich and complex it is, so we can only describe it imperfectly. However, it can inspire and enliven, as artists of all fields reveal. To this worldview Giribone counters a very different and less reassuring version. The most acceptable, perhaps, is Camus's absurdity, "this destroyed, mindless world in which the protagonist of the story 'The Stranger' moves, initiating actions that have become almost autonomous, unconnected to one another." Sartre's vision of this region is even harsher: in the novel "The Disgust", objects are deprived of their concept, their definition, "monstrous and collapsed like Dali's soft clocks" they lie around [2]. In both Camus and Sartre, there is nothing left that could organize or construct the world, that is, it has no meaning.

Giribone supposes that the inaccessible and chaotic world that precedes meaning, that unfolds before meaning is added, corresponds to the archaic universe of the not-yet-speaking child or the madman. Invisible and latently present, it is felt as a potential threat. Only the cartography of language creates something like reassurance. For him, there are two ways of looking at the same area: when things lose their familiarity, the world dissolves. The feeling of the uncanny arises. It is connected with the fear of the loss of meaningfulness. Meaning is not permanently inscribed in things, meaning is not the thing as such, it is really only a frame. Meaning is basically that which makes sense, and in this capacity it can be perforated, annulled, disappear.

But, according to Giribone, there is another, more confidence inspiring version of this disappearance. In this other constellation, the human is not swept away, for he remains outside the potentially frightening spectacle – that is the comic scene. The frame stiffens, the meaning it carries disappears through excessive materialization, but it remains as a horizon. It is not questioned in its function, in its essence, if the great instances that shape our perception are preserved: the constancy of the observing human being, the world he constructs, and the meaning that language gives it. These instances, however, may falter, thus proving fragile. The laughter and the uncanny show us the same characters, refer to the same area, only they suggest different ways of seeing: One makes us laugh tears, the other shows us its threatening grimace.

10.1 Framework in AI

Different ways of looking at the world, frames that suggest contexts, also play an important role in AI. We have talked about the representation of knowledge from different points of view in Chap. 5. In doing so, we had discussed various formalisms that could be used to represent knowledge formally and logically. In a small example in Fig. 5.1, a tiny section of knowledge about different kinds of living beings was represented. If one wants to use such knowledge in an AI system, very large knowledge bases have to be consulted. This can be thought of as in our small example, except that the number of concepts and the relations between them are immense. For example, Google's *Knowledge Graph* currently contains about 70 billion facts; another commercially available knowledge base from Cyc[3] contains significantly fewer facts and statements – about 7 million – but is carefully compiled, sometimes by hand. One problem with automatically processing such vast amounts of knowledge is finding appropriate information. For this purpose, Cyc has divided the knowledge base into so-called micro-theories belonging to individual domains or sub-domains; the processing of knowledge should remain within these micro-theories – the micro-theory forms a framework. Such frameworks for representing knowledge have already been introduced by

---

[3] www.cyc.com, accessed 11/2/2018.

Marvin Minsky, one of the doyens of the field. In [7], Minsky proposes to organize knowledge into *frames*. Such a frame does not only define the meaning of a fact, rather it defines a kind of scenario. Minsky gives a little story as an example:

Jane was invited to Jack's birthday party.
She wondered if he would like a kite.
She went to her room and shook her piggy bank.
It made no sound.

To understand this text, one could now look up the meaning of children's birthday party in a dictionary. One then finds, for example, in the Duden[4] "Noun, masculine – birthday party arranged for children on the occasion of a child's birthday." But to understand the second sentence of the story, this definition is not enough. One must know that to a birthday party one brings a present – and this just might be a kite. Minsky now proposes a frame for a child's birthday party, which contains so-called *slots,* such as DRESS, PRESENT, GAMES, and so on. These slots can then be filled with concrete details from the story; for PRESENT, kites could be entered, and for GAMES, for example, pot banging would be a suitable filler. A similar approach was proposed in story understanding by Roger Shank [8]. Here the idea is to prescribe prototypical actions in certain situation by a *script. For* example, when a person enters a restaurant, the corresponding script is activated. Here, so-called roles are now provided, such as the waiter, the cook, or the cashier. Likewise, typical processes are predefined, such as waiting until a table is assigned, ordering and waiting for the food, and so on until paying and leaving the restaurant. Such a typical sequence of events can now be used for text comprehension by trying to find the necessary roles and actions in the text, and by matching text and script as much as possible. One problem with using this approach, however, is finding the most appropriate script possible. The individual scripts contain a kind of header with information about necessary prerequisites for their use. For example, the restaurant script may require that the protagonist is hungry (or has an appointment) and that he has enough money. In practice, this will very often be the case, so many scripts will need to be checked for applicability, resulting in a large search space.

If we are talking about typical and recurring processes here, the idea of a plan is obvious. In AI research, formalisms for planning had to be developed when people tried to design autonomous robots. One of the first robotic

---

[4] www.duden.de, accessed 10/23/2018.

systems was Shakey [9], whom we have already mentioned in Chap. 3. Its development is therefore considered a milestone in AI history because it was the first time that a formalism was used to define and process plans. Anyone who has ever cooked according to a recipe is familiar with the concept of a plan – a cooking recipe can very well be conceived as such. It lays out a sequence of actions that the cook works through in order. Thus, an action might be "boil water," followed by the action "add rice to the water," and finally "simmer gently for 15 min." The author of the recipe assumes that the cook can perform each action and is aware of its effect. However, in order for a robot to be able to perform each action, it is necessary to formulate very precisely what the necessary conditions are. For example, for "boil water" a pot of water must be available, a stove flame must be free and turned on, and the pot must be placed on it. But this action[5] also has an effect, namely that the stove flame is no longer free and that the water is hot. All this has to be formalized; for Shakey, the planning formalism Strips was developed for this purpose. One has a description of the world; in our kitchen scenario, for example, the position of the utensils, the stove, the refrigerator, but also the available food together with where it is stored must be described. For this purpose, one can use exactly the logical knowledge representation formalisms as introduced in Chap. 5. Now, when describing actions, a logic formalism cannot be used directly – the reason for this is due to the so-called frame problem. As indicated in the kitchen example, the effect of an action must be described; to do this, it must be specified which properties of the environment are changed, e.g. that the flame of the stove on which the pot for boiling the water is placed is no longer free. In logic, however, it would also be necessary to describe which properties in the whole kitchen remain unchanged, e.g. that the butter is still in the fridge afterwards, the table is still in the same place, and the window is still closed, and so on and so forth. So we find here exactly the framing problem of this chapter: the frame in which individual actions are applicable and have effect must be marked out. In Strips, this is solved by an arrangement: for each action, you have a "delete list" and an "add list". The former contains the properties that no longer apply after the action has been executed, the latter the properties that apply anew afterwards. Everything that is not contained in the two lists remains unchanged. – The two lists together with this agreement thus span the framework for the action.

Having discussed frames in knowledge processing and planning so far, we will now also address the use of frames in modeling humor. There are indeed attempts to have humor and jokes understood or generated by AI systems; the

---

[5] In fact, it is again a sequence of actions, namely "grab pot", "fill with water" and "put on free stove flame". Here it is simplified as one action.

term "computational humor" has become established for this work. Here, attempts are made to model or formalize the mechanism of humor on the basis of psychological and linguistic theories. What most of these approaches have in common is that they assume that humour arises from misplacement, in that two opposing or merely overlapping scripts come into play as interpretations of a text. So, for example, if a person who has the role of a waiter in a restaurant script, and is there assigned to direct seats, take the order, bring the food, or cash up, sits down in a text and eats the food he has just brought himself, this could be an indication of a joke. Two incompatible roles, that of the waiter and that of the eating guest, are used simultaneously in a script.

One can distinguish two different directions of research in this area: the detection of jokes or humor in a text and the generation of jokes. For the former, classical machine learning approaches, as we described in Chap. 5 on artificial neural networks, can be used. One trains the system with a large number of texts, indicating for each text whether it represents a joke or not. The system trained in this way will eventually recognize whether a new text presented is a joke – it has solved a classification task. However, the system does not know why a text is funny. This is probably why it is worthwhile to use "deep" linguistic methods when recognizing jokes or humor. Here, one tries to capture the meaning of the text using linguistic formalisms, thereby revealing different possible interpretations; if these are very contradictory, this is an indication of a joke. The challenge here is that linguistic analysis alone is not sufficient – a great deal of knowledge must also be involved in understanding the text, similar to what we discussed for processing everyday knowledge in cognitive computing in Chap. 5. We will discuss linguistic methods in detail later in Chap. 12.

One can proceed differently with the generation of jokes. For this, you can specify certain joke patterns, which are then instantiated with different people and objects.

We have seen that the principles of these AI approaches are related to those of the authors covered in this chapter.

10.2 Summary

This chapter has discussed that a frame exists around a particular context, event, or piece of knowledge; if a story, description, or event leaves this frame, we experience the event as funny. If we lose reference to the frame, or if it is damaged, we are unsettled or frightened. With Bergson we saw that automatic or unnaturally mechanical things in certain situations go beyond the frame of expected natural behavior and thus become comic. Giribone showed that the intrusion of a foreign object into the frame or alienation of the frame can be unsettling. In AI, on the other hand, frames have been used to organize knowledge; we used Minsky's "frames" or Shank's "scripts" as examples here. These frames, in contrast to the philosophical theories cited, are mainly used to avoid running into the void when using knowledge and after searching for appropriate contexts, that is, to get help in the search, so to speak.

In planning, however, the situation is contrary; here the frame for each action of a robot must be explicitly formulated. The frame on which the action has an effect must be explicitly defined here, and therefore leads to a complication of the plan rather than a simplification.

Under the catchword "computational humor", however, there is also research in AI to model the comical or uncanny. For example, when using a script, new objects or persons are introduced that are not intended there. Or one uses objects or persons of a script à la Sartre or Dali in a way that runs counter to the script definition.

Should the predictions of the transhumanists (see Chap. 3) come true and we are facing the Singularity, i.e. when AI has created its own world and humanity no longer plays a role on this planet, AI systems will also enjoy artificial humour.

References

1. Bergson H (2011) Das Lachen: Le rire. Ein Essay über die Bedeutung des Komischen, Bd 622. Meiner Verlag, Hamburg
2. Giribone J-L (2007) Le comique et l'inquiétante étrangeté: Bergson et Freud. Cahiers critiques de thérapie familiale et de pratiques de réseaux 2:17–37
3. Freud S (1948) Das Unheimliche: Aufsätze zur Literatur, Bd 4. Fischer, Frankfurt
4. Bateson G (1983) Ökologie des Geistes, Bd 6. Suhrkamp, Frankfurt
5. Kafka F (1998) Der Process. Reclam Universal-Bibliothek, Stuttgart
6. Bergson H (1934) Denken und schöpferisches Werden. Libri, Hamburg
7. Minsky M (1981) A framework for representing knowledge. In: Haugeland J (Hrsg) Mind design: philosophy, psychology, artificial intelligence. MIT Press, Cambridge, S. 95–128
8. Schank RC, Abelson R (1977) Scripts, goals, plans, and understanding. Erlbaum, Hillsdale
9. Nilsson NJ (1984) Shakey the robot. Technical report, SRI International Menlo Park CA

11

Consciousness

Abstract We pursue the question of what constitutes consciousness and find what we are looking for in the phenomenologists. They place the body, which perceives the things around it, at the centre of their considerations. The localization of consciousness is illustrated by the theatrical metaphor. The modelling of consciousness in AI could help to deal more efficiently with the quantities of information.

". . . und hab ihn so weit gebracht dass er mich gebeten hat ja zu sagen und zuerst hab ich gar keine Antwort gegeben hab bloß rausgeschaut aufs Meer und über den Himmel ich musste an so viele Sachen denken von denen er gar nichts wusste (...) ja und die ganzen komischen kleinen Straßen und Gässchen und rosa und blauen und gelben Häuser und die Rosengärten und der Jasmin und die Geranien und Kaktusse und Gibraltar als kleines Mädchen wo ich eine Blume des Berges war ja wie ich mir die Rose ins Haar gesteckt hab wie die andalusischen Mädchen immer machten oder soll ich eine rote tragen ja und wie er mich hat unter der maurischen Mauer und ich habe gedacht na schön er so gut wie jeder andere und hab ihn mit den Augen gebeten er soll doch noch mal fragen ja und dann hat er mich gefragt ob ich will ja sag ja meine Bergblume und ich hab ihm zuerst die Arme um

© The Author(s), under exclusive license to Springer Fachmedien Wiesbaden GmbH, part of Springer Nature 2023
U. Barthelmeß, U. Furbach, *A Different Look at Artificial Intelligence*, https://doi.org/10.1007/978-3-658-38474-6_11

den Hals gelegt und ihn zu mir niedergezogen dass er meine Brüste fühlen konnte wie sie dufteten ja und das Herz ging mir wie verrückt ich hab ja gesagt ja ich will Ja [1]."[1]

The novel "Ulysses" by James Joyce (1882–1941) is considered a prime example of the use of the narrative technique of the stream of consciousness. It covers the course of a single day of the protagonist Leopold Bloom. The narrator describes what happens to him or goes through his mind on that day. In the passage from the final chapter quoted here, the first-person narrator Molly Bloom recalls, in a kind of half-sleep, the day on which Leopold Bloom proposed to her.

This technique is about letting the character's consciousness speak for itself, without the structuring intervention of a narrative instance becoming visible, in order to create a protocol-like reproduction of the contents of consciousness, to depict consciousness uncensored in the original. James Joyce was not the only one who tried to depict the "truth" of our being, the incessant "noise" in the brain, as authentically as possible.

To observe the workings of the stream of consciousness on oneself, think of the attempts to shake off that noise when one wants to fall asleep. Snatches of thoughts emerge as if from nowhere, working their way into consciousness, even if we reject them because we don't want to deal with them: Topics of everyday life, to-do lists, thoughts that have been left lying around, burdensome feelings, worries. ... The body writhes under their weight, trying to remedy the situation by changing it – usually in vain. Cunning parades, such as the famous counting of sheep or the mental walking of certain rooms, apartments, running routes, etc., are usually seen through by the noise, it can not be so easily dismissed. At some point one wakes up and wonders: it has worked after all to push away the noise and enter the realm of sleep and dreaming. We missed the threshold between waking and sleeping, the border

---

[1] ... and I got him to the point where he asked me to say yes and at first I didn't give any answer I just looked out at the sea and across the sky I had to think of so many things he didn't know anything about (…) yes and all the funny little streets and alleys and pink and blue and yellow houses and rose gardens and the jasmine and geraniums and cactuses and Gibraltar when he said yes.) yes and all the funny little streets and alleys and pink and blue and yellow houses and the rose gardens and the jasmine and the geraniums and the cactuses and Gibraltar as a little girl where I was a flower of the mountain yes and how I put the rose in my hair like the Andalusian girls always did or should I wear a red one yes and how he took me under the Moorish wall and I thought well well, he's nice. Wall and I thought well he is as good as anyone and I asked him with my eyes to ask again yes and then he asked me if I want yes say yes my mountain flower and I first put my arms around his neck and pulled him down to me so that he could feel my breasts as they smelled yes and my heart went like crazy I said yes yes I want yes.

crossing. Something within us had willed us to fall asleep, to descend into the realm of the unconscious, ignoring the weariness of our flesh. It wouldn't let us shut down, kept us awake, and forced us to stay awake and connected to the world. Here we try to trace the nature of consciousness.

11.1 Qualia

In connection with the discussion of body and mind in Chap. 3, we have left out an important aspect, namely the feeling and experiencing of the environment through our sensors, which are, after all, part of the body. When we feel a surface with our fingertips, we have a very specific sensation that is triggered by the sensors in our skin; when we look at a colored surface, a very specific sensation is triggered in us; this inner state can feel different with a rich red than with a cool blue. It is important to note that this "feeling" is subjective – we experience it without knowing whether it feels the same way in our counterpart.

In philosophy this effect, the feeling of a mental state, is called "qualia". The discussion of qualia is central to the question of the nature of consciousness. Qualia conditions introspection in certain mental states; the question is whether qualia and consciousness are material, that is, physically tangible. Leibniz already described a thought experiment on this: Let us imagine that we inspect a model of a brain, we can see in it the transmission and processing of stimuli, quite similar to what we have described in the sections on artificial neural networks. We know how stimulus processing works in the eye and further down to the various regions in the brain; we have described this in detail in Chap. 7. But nowhere in the brain can we localize how it feels to see the color red. With all the knowledge we have about the neurobiological nature of the brain, we find no trace of qualia or consciousness. Henri Bergson already formulated something similar in [2]. He describes the processing of stimuli in our nervous system, using neuro-biological reasoning to justify that there is no need for any special agency – i.e. consciousness – in the brain. Bergson describes the brain and the structure of the nervous system as a stimulus-processing system. A sensory organ receives a stimulus and can immediately transmit it to muscles to trigger an action. In other cases, the stimulus signal from the sensory organ is first sent to the brain, from where it can be relayed to muscles. "Ich verstehe nicht und werde nie verstehen, dass sie (die periphere Reizung) dort die wundersame Kraft schöpfen soll, sich in eine Vorstellung von Dingen zu verwandeln; ...".[2] argues Bergson. Rather, he conceives of the brain as a kind of telephone exchange (note the reference to the technological advances of his time), whose job it is to make or break connections.

11.2 The Role of the Body

The philosopher Merleau-Ponty pursued the question of the phenomenon of consciousness in a very special way in his work "Phénoménologie de la perception", Phenomenology of Perception (1945) [3].

Maurice Merleau-Ponty was born on March 14, 1908

in Rochefort-sur-Mer, a small town in the southwest of France. Since relatively little is known about his private life, as Gerhard Danzer regrets in his book on the philosopher [4], we will limit ourselves here to his career as a scientist.

After high school, he attended the Ecole Normale Supérieure, an elite school in Paris, where he made the acquaintance of Claude Levi-Strauss, Jean-Paul Sartre and Simone de Beauvoir. With the latter two, he formed an almost life-long friendship. He was mainly concerned with philosophy. His teachers and role models included Bergson and – after a few years as a high school philosophy teacher – Husserl, the founder of the philosophical movement of phenomenology, who lectured at the Sorbonne. Like these two philosophical models, who linked their philosophical theories with other sciences and the arts, Merleau-Ponty also moved into non-philosophical terrain such as Gestalt and developmental psychology, medicine, linguistics, painting and literature.

He first emancipated himself from Christian existentialism by turning to communist ideas, and finally distanced himself from communism because he did not want to be bound by party politics and he rejected totalitarian systems, which led, among other things, to a break with Sartre, who was close to communism.

His doctorate with the work "Phenomenology of Perception" launches his university career. First he was professor of child psychology in Lyon, then he lectured in education science at the Sorbonne. Finally, like Henri Bergson before him, he held the renowned philosophy chair at the Collège de France, where he researched and taught until his sudden death in 1961.

In his inaugural lecture, "Eloge de la Philosophie" (In Praise of Philosophy), he addresses the role of the philosopher, drawing in particular on Bergson's attitude: "Die Beziehung zwischen dem Philosophen und dem Sein ist nicht eine frontale Beziehung zwischen einem Zuschauer und einem Schauspiel; sie ist vielmehr die einer Mittäterschaft."[5][3] This is already his core thesis that the philosopher as a human being is to be included in his philosophical reflections.

---

[2] I do not understand, and never will understand, that it (peripheral stimulation) should draw there the miraculous power of transforming itself into a conception of things; ...

[3] The relation between the philosopher and being is not a frontal relation between a spectator and a spectacle; it is rather that of complicity.

"Philosophie heißt in Wahrheit, von Neuem lernen, die Welt zu sehen."[3][4] Merleau-Ponty defies traditional philosophical theories and seeks a new way of seeing the world. He looks around him and states – seemingly naively – that the world already exists before philosophical reflection and that this perception is through the living subject. A point of view outside the living subject would only be accessible to an absolute God.

Merleau-Ponty frees himself from the Descartesian distinction between the realm of meaning and signs (language and ideas) and the realm of physical objects (the space of things and the body) and links human experience and cognition itself to space and spatial experience. Pure observation, like pure consciousness or pure communication, is abstract and impractical against the background of the bodily interconnectedness of all expressions of life with the world. The fact of bodily presence in the world cannot simply be denied. Reality can therefore not be created, but only described.

The living subject, the body that experiences itself in the world, perceives, and in this perception consciousness takes its origin. Perception, and thus the action it triggers, therefore occupies a primary position. The world is not what I think, but what I live [3]. Merleau-Ponty speaks of the body's "being-to-the-world" (être au monde). The body is not reduced to its bio-physiological phenomena, but it forms a unity with the world it perceives. The philosopher who eliminates his own perspective, who ignores himself as a self-perceiving subject, thereby obscures the insight that it is precisely this perspective that makes knowledge possible. He loses touch with his origin, with natural, factual life and action. As a human being, he deals with the structured world in that stimulus and reaction, which can never be completely separated, are always formed anew.

Man does not react to isolated stimuli or construct them in his consciousness, but forms in his body structures of absorbed and transformed entities of complex nature that influence him and in which he participates [6]. Merleau-Ponty demonstrates this with the simple perception of a football pitch:

Der Fußballplatz ist für den Spieler in Aktion kein ‚Objekt', d. h. der ideelle Zielpunkt, der eine unendliche Mannigfaltigkeit perspektivischer Ansichten zuläßt und in all seinen erscheinungsmäßigen Umformungen den gleichen Wert behauptet. Er ist von Kraftlinien durchzogen (‚Seitenlinien', Linien, die den ‚Strafraum' abgrenzen) – in Abschnitte gegliedert (z. B. die ‚Lücken' zwischen den Gegnern), die eine Aktion von ganz bestimmter Art herbeirufen, sie auslösen und tragen, gleichsam ohne Wissen des Spielers. Der Spielplatz ist

---

[4] Philosophy really means seeing the world from a new perspective.

ihm nicht gegeben, sondern er ist gegenwärtig als der immanente Zielpunkt seiner praktischen Intentionen; der Spieler bezieht ihn in seinen Körper mit ein und spürt beispielsweise die Richtung des ‚Tores' ebenso unmittelbar wie die Vertikale und Horizontale seines eigenen Leibes [7].[5]

Fehler! Linkreferenz ungültig. Merleau-Ponty's new view consists in the fact that he seeks a "Zwischenreich" [6] between the empirical sciences, which trust only the power of the sensual, and the idealistic philosophies, which see only a sense-giving consciousness. His "Zwischenreich" concretizes both: the sensual, that is, empirically perceived, and sense, the meaning creating. It is also the key in considerations of art and language theory (we will discuss the latter in Chap. 12 on language), when it is a matter of the relationship between the expressor, the artist or speaker, and the expressed, the work of art or language.

While Merleau-Ponty distanced himself from various traditional philosophical schools, he did use some tools as foundations for his philosophy. Four key methodological concepts characterize his philosophy of life: dialectics, ambiguity, phenomenology, psychology.

Following Hegel's dialectic, he sees man as a natural and cultural being in a dialectical field of tension: man with his body is part of the material world and with his consciousness at the same time its observer. The world and human beings are characterized by opposites. The world, being, can only be experienced through the subjective consciousness of man. The latter sets out again and again to seek the truth, which he can never fully internalize: "Das Ende einer Philosophie ist die Erzählung ihres Anfangs." [8][6]

In the immediate vicinity of dialectics is the concept of ambiguity. It has a decisive influence on Merleau-Ponty's philosophical stance. It means ambiguity and refers to the fact that phenomena such as body, mind, art, life have something ambiguous about them. The body is on the one hand a thing and on the other hand a carrier of the ego. An example of this ambiguity is that of the hands touching themselves, the experience of "touching the touched". As in a conundrum, there is no one-sided resolution, but rather the endurance of the open. It is through this act of holding oneself in balance that one does

---

[5] For the player in action, the football pitch is not an 'object', i.e. the ideal target point that allows for an infinite variety of perspective views and asserts the same value in all its appearances. It is criss-crossed by lines of force ('side lines', lines demarcating the 'penalty area') – divided into sections (e.g. the 'gaps' between the opponents), which summon an action of a very definite kind, trigger it and carry it, as it were without the knowledge of the player. The playground is not given to him, but is present as the immanent goal of his practical intentions; the player incorporates it into his body and feels, for example, the direction of the 'goal' as directly as the vertical and horizontal of his own body.

[6] The end of a philosophy is the narration of its beginning.

justice to the ambiguity of the world. Therefore, a researcher must acknowledge this ambiguity and adopt different research and observation standpoints. Gerhard Danzer cites psychosomatics as an example, where two disparate entities 'soma' and 'psyche' are harnessed before a common cart [9]. Patients suffered from both physical and psychological disorders, and therapists should be able to take both aspects into account (see also Chap. 3).

To the view of man, who in an ambiguous sense is part of the world and consciousness of it at the same time, corresponds the idea of a consciousness that is always a consciousness of something and not an empty container that is filled with things of the world. It manifests itself only in man's contact with the world. This conception is based on the term "intentionality" coined by Husserl.[7]

If consciousness is always consciousness of something, the question of the something arises. It is the appearance of a thing, the phenomenon (phainomenon). According to Plato, however, this describes only the surface and transient side of the thing; what is permanent about it is the essence or idea of the thing. While the concrete world is thus devalued in favor of the world of ideas, Husserl takes the opposite path. He wants to penetrate "To the things themselves!". By things he understands the world with all phenomena, however small and insignificant they may appear. One should encounter them as unprejudiced as possible and describe them unadulterated. Therefore, in order to know an object, everything must be bracketed that could hinder the knowledge of the essence of the object. This was called by Husserl "phenomenological reduction" or "epoché" (restraint of judgment in Stoic philosophy). The contemplating self is also to purify itself of all judgment and suspend the concrete self in order to become an absolute self. One can see that the premises for approaching the essence of things are difficult to fulfill. Given the difficulty of such an endeavor – can one, after all, provide an absolutely clear view of the world? – phenomenology was seen more as a style or attitude towards things. We will talk about the so-called priming effect in connection with this observation below.

Merleau-Ponty concludes, that the most important doctrine of reduction is thus that of the impossibility of complete reduction [3]. The philosopher is also always part of the world he explores and reflects upon. This relation to the world he calls, as mentioned above, "être-au-monde", "being-to-the-world". Hence he modifies "epoché" and calls only for an attitude of wonder on the part of the philosopher about man and the world. Wondering implies restraint

---

[7] We find this idea reflected in psychologist Bernard Baars' model of theatre, which we discuss below.

in reflective contemplation and a break with habitual familiarity with the world. He shifts the recognition of a being, the so-called "Wesensschau", from the factual to the qualitative, from the that to the how. Thus, the preface to "Phänomenologie der Wahrnehmung" states: "Zur Welt seiend, sind wir verurteilt zum Sinn, und nichts können wir tun oder sagen, was in der Geschichte nicht seinen Namen fände."[8]

We exist in life and struggle for truth from that position. The process of understanding takes place in a constant interaction between the examiner and the object examined. The observer, and in particular his or her body, interacts with the world. Analogously, this is called in Nouvelle AI "situatedness".

The body-subject, the term for the place of the foundation of man in the world, is the mediator of mind and body-object.[9] Consciousness and body-object cannot be separated, but unite in the body-subject. It is the medium to the world and anchorage in the world. Gestalt and depth psychology also grasp the human being as a whole. Freud proceeds like a hermeneuticist when he reads the messages of his patients from the page, i.e. from their bodies. The bodies contain traces of memory, signs of the past, which their authors cannot decipher without hel.

Man is part of nature and part of the meaning that lies within it. Our attitude towards it is both natural, insofar as our body-subject comes from nature, and cultural, insofar as we draw something from nature. For Merleau-Ponty's concept of nature, Schelling's philosophy of nature is decisive: the latter's core idea was that not only the spirit but also nature is capable of developing autonomously, and thus made it possible for man to emancipate himself from it. Its history is that of development to higher and higher autonomous levels. In inorganic nature it is the crystallizations that exhibit self-structuring; organic nature has a higher degree of freedom because of its self-production, and in man creative productivity comes to itself. In this context, Danzer also refers to Bergson's "élan vital" (see Chap. 4), which we seek to grasp through intuition.

There is an interrelationship between the human being, who needs the sounding board of the world to think and feel, and the world, which acquires a context and meaning through the human being's consciousness. His individual biographical and social makeup determines the extent of his openness

---

[8] Being to the world, we are condemned to sense, and nothing can we do or say that would not find its name in history.

[9] The body-object is that which can be objectively grasped, it refers to the human body from a biological/physical/medical perspective, while the body-subject is not accessible to such objectification procedures, it refers to the human body in a perspective that goes beyond scientific aspects. One *has* a body-object, while one *is* a body-subject.

to the world. Just as there is the geometric space of things, there is the "anthropological space" of man, which is always reconstituted as it is modulated by the particular culture, social environment, individual perspective, psychological state. Danzer mentions patients whose sense of space is severely impaired and whose subjective space is characterized by eeriness, loneliness, emotional coldness, and lifelessness [4].[10]

Analogous to anthropological space, there is anthropological time: "Neben den zwischen mir und allen Dingen bestehenden physischen und geometrischen Abstand verbindet ein erlebter Abstand mich den Dingen, die für mich zählen und existieren, und verbindet sie untereinander. Dieser Abstand ist von Augenblick zu Augenblick das Maß und die Weite meines Lebens."[11] [3]: everyone lives in his individual subjective time, which can be equated with Bergson's durée (see Chap. 4). Time is not a stream, but the way we live our existence. The body-subject is the order-giving basis for everything we do, for our perceptions, contacts and relationships to other people.

11.3 The Theatre Model

So let us follow the phenomenologists and agree that there is no material consciousness. But how then is consciousness to be explained or localized? A well-accepted explanation in psychology comes from Bernard J. Baars in the form of a so-called "theatre model" [10]. Such theatre models have a long tradition in philosophy and psychology. Already Plato treats a kind of theatre in his allegory of the cave: prisoners in a cave perceive objects from the world outside the cave only as shadows on a wall; this wall is the only thing the persons in the cave can perceive, the voices from outside are reflected in the cave, so that it appears to the cave dwellers that the shadows can speak. Philosopher and cognitive scientist Daniel Dennett coined the term Cartesian theatre; we imagine a place in the brain that has something of a mental screen or stage, there images are presented to our mind's eye. Everything that happens in this Cartesian theatre is conscious to us – in fact, there are experiments from cognitive research that prove that we manipulate mental objects in certain situations. For example, we can imagine objects and mentally rotate them in space,

---

[10] Parallels could be drawn here with Giribone's framing hypothesis concerning the uncanny (see Chap. 10)

[11] In addition to the physical and geometrical distance that exists between me and all things, an experienced distance connects me to the things that count and exist for me, and connects them to each other. This distance is, from moment to moment, the measure and expanse of my life.

for example to make a comparison with another object. Or we can move around in an imagined space, as we did in our little experiment on spatial imagining in Chap. 5. However, there is no place in the brain where this stage or screen can be determined. Baars' theatre model, which illustrates the so-called global workspace theory, also models this aspect.

According to Baars, we have the following parts of the theatre:

The Stage

It can be conceived of as the working memory. It contains propositional and pictorial knowledge and is accessible for a limited time; after some time it disappears and remains in the dark. The "active" elements on stage are present, such as sensory input, memorized items (e.g. phone numbers), images we imagine, or objects we are using or plan to use – all of which we are aware of.

The Headlight

It directs attention to what is happening on stage, to a part of the stage. This attention can be directed arbitrarily or involuntarily. We can imagine the supermarket on the way home from work together with the planned purchases and "light" them.

The Actors

The individual elements of working memory, that is, the actors on stage, are usually in competition with each other. They try to get the attention, to get into the circle of light of the spotlight.

The Context Behind the Scenes

Events on stage are of course also determined by actors backstage, just as our experiences are influenced by unconscious contexts. The directing of attention is mostly spontaneous and unconscious, as if commands from offstage control the spotlight. We have already discussed in our discussion of the visual process that an important part of visual perception occurs unconsciously, and contexts play a significant role in this. For when objects are to be recognized and classified, memories and experiences come into play.

The Spectators

The huge big audience represents the long-term memory, a set of specialized knowledge that is not conscious. The work of navigating this long-term memory is mostly unconscious and probably highly parallelized.

This theatre metaphor can also model some aspects of learning. Consciousness opens the door, so to speak, to a vast memory, and here the process of learning also plays a role. Consciousness points to a particular aspect to be learned, and this in itself triggers rules and procedures that allow us to learn. In the theatre it is the stage with its spotlight that brings a certain event to the fore – the learning then happens in the dark auditorium, that is where all the unconscious learning procedures are. We have already dealt several times with such learning procedures in the form of neural networks; here it is the triggering of the procedure, the provision of the inputs to the procedure, that is of interest. For example, it seems impossible to take in those words you just read without certain memories or bits of knowledge coming into the spotlight of attention. The so-called "priming effect" also plays an important role here: if you show test subjects pictures of objects, e.g. a loaf of bread or a letterbox, for a very short time, they are correctly classified in 40% of all cases. However, if the subject sees a picture of a kitchen beforehand, the correctness of the loaf of bread increases to 80% of all cases. All objects that do not match the kitchen are still only correctly recognized with a probability of 40%.

This priming effect also clearly shows that our conscious mind is an important tool to navigate through the vast amount of knowledge, images and experiences we have at our disposal at any given time. Our short-term memory can only make a few morsels of knowledge available at a time, the rest must be retrieved from the unconscious. There, many unconscious processes run in parallel, controlling our bodily functions, taking in sensory input, processing it, and controlling the body's locomotor system. Our brain copes with this by only illuminating the relevant part and bringing it on stage. We talked in the knowledge representation section about how hard it is to process general knowledge as efficiently as we humans can. In Chap. 5, we had given an example from natural language question and answer systems. Finding the right answer here was simply trivial for humans, whereas an artificial system finds it extraordinarily difficult to do so, precisely because it has to select the correct, relevant parts from the huge knowledge base. This is the subject of current research in this area – the problem is described in detail in [11]. The theatre model described above has also been used to "let an AI system's mind wander" – in the same way that we sometimes let our minds wander and, for example, while thinking about a snowstorm, come up with the topic of a refrigerator and immediately land in another step on our next week's shopping. In this vein, an AI system designed for rational and logical reasoning has been enabled to let its "thoughts" wander freely across a large knowledge base, much like the spotlight in Baars' theater model. This has already resulted in extremely creative combinations of knowledge in initial experiments. The difficulty, however, is evaluating which connections are so interesting that they are worth pursuing. This evaluation should ultimately be carried out by the AI system itself, thus introducing a kind of creative step into the course of a problem-solving process [12].

11.4 Consciousness in AI

The emphasis on consciousness can be found again and again in the philosophical discussion of artificial intelligence. We had talked in detail about the Turing test as a criterion for AI in Chap. 2. The philosopher Thomas Metzinger even reformulates the Turing test with the help of consciousness [13]. This criterion, which he calls the Metzinger test, states that we should not treat a system as an independent object until "it advocates its own theory of consciousness, i.e., when it begins to enter the discussion of artificial consciousness with arguments of its own." While Metzinger cites a number of criteria necessary for the development of consciousness – these include, for example, situatedness in a dynamic environment and experienced presence – he does not specify a test in the sense of Turing's imitation game. Rather, his point is to emphasize that we should not even attempt to create a "postbiotic consciousness." Roughly speaking, such a system would also feel suffering, so we would have created additional suffering, which, according to Metzinger, should be avoided at all costs in academic research.

On the other hand, a certain form of consciousness – or let's call it self-assessment at this point – is certainly necessary to make systems act intelligently. Let's take the cognitive computing system Watson, which has been mentioned several times, as an example. At the beginning of 2011, Watson had to defeat the two record champions Ken Jennings and Brad Rutter in a three-day tournament on the very popular quiz show Jeopardy! in the USA. Watson must have very good general knowledge to do this, because after all, the questions can come from many different areas of knowledge. Watson also has to understand the natural language questions, which often include puns and innuendo on Jeopardy![12] It was an amazing competition – especially since

---

[12] Actually, they are not questions, but answers, and the players have to find the corresponding questions.

Watson had to be fast, since the players are under severe time pressure here. In the video recordings of the quiz, you can see Watson's answer candidates after each question, along with a confidence measure that the system uses to judge whether the answer is good enough. It is quite common for Watson to have a correct candidate answer, but not name it because he is not completely sure. This confidence measure is composed of very many different components that played a role in finding the candidate answers. In another natural language system that answers questions based on Wikipedia, the confidence measure is formed using various syntactic, but also semantic criteria [14]. Here, no pre-defined function is used for the calculation, rather the measure is learned by machine learning methods, so that the self-assessment procedure can also change and improve over time.

Such a property certainly cannot already be called consciousness, but it seems to me a clear step in the direction demanded by Metzinger. Metzinger, however, would distinguish between self-models with and without conscious-ness [15] and would presumably grant Watson only an unconscious self-model.

But why is it important for an AI system to have consciousness at all? In the motivation and introduction of the theatre model, Baars argues that con-sciousness gives our brains the ability to deal with vast amounts of knowledge and information. When needed, the spotlight activates the appropriate parts of memory and brings them to the attention of the stage. The priming effect described above provides impressive evidence of this. Now such a mechanism could be useful in AI systems. We had argued that question-answering sys-tems require large amounts of knowledge. Storing the knowledge is not a significant problem here; there are now cheap and fast techniques to manage knowledge. Many sources of knowledge are also public and accessible via cloud services. These are huge collections of natural language texts and images, but structured knowledge is also available in large quantities and can be used by the reasoning mechanisms of AI systems. The problem here, however, is finding the appropriate parts of the knowledge; this is precisely where model-ing consciousness can hopefully help.

11.5 Summary

Starting with a description of the concept of qualia, we have shown that in philosophy the phenomenologists, especially Merleau-Ponty, made important contributions to the nature of consciousness. Regarding a modeling of con-sciousness, we were able to draw on the psychologist Baars' theatre model, and we discussed that this metaphor can also be valuable in the development of AI systems. Baars' motivation for developing his model was to master the immense amount of memories, knowledge, and experiences that we have at our disposal extremely efficiently all the time. We have discussed that this can also be particularly useful for AI systems that need to master large amounts of knowledge. Moreover, based on such an understanding of consciousness, it is also quite possible to speak of consciousness in artificial systems.

References

1. Joyce J (1996) Ulysses. Suhrkamp, Berlin
2. Bergson H (2001) Materie und Gedächtnis. Eine Abhandlung über die Beziehung zwischen Körper und Geist. Verlag Felix Meiner, Berlin
3. Merleau-Ponty M (1966) Phänomenologie der Wahrnehmung. De Gruyter, Berlin
4. Danzer G (2003) Merleau-Ponty. Ein Philosoph auf der Such nach dem Sinn. Kulturverlag Kadmos, Berlin
5. Merleau-Ponty M (1973) Vorlesungen I. De Gruyter, Berlin
6. Bermes C (2012) Maurice Merleau-Ponty zur Einführung. Junius Verlag, Hamburg
7. Merleau-Ponty M (1976) Die Struktur des Verhaltens. De Gruyter, Berlin
8. Merleau-Ponty M (2004) Das Sichtbare und das Unsichtbare. Fink, München
9. Danzer G (2011) Wer sind wir? Springer, Berlin
10. Baars BJ (1997) In the theatre of consciousness. Global workspace theory, a rigorous scientific theory of consciousness. J Conscious Stud 4(4):292–309
11. Furbach U, Schon C (2016) Commonsense reasoning meets theorem proving. In: Klusch M, Unland R, Shehory O, Pokahr A, Ahrndt S (Hrsg) Multiagent system technologies – 14th German conference, MATES 2016, Klagenfurt, Österreich, September 27–30, 2016. Proceedings, volume 9872 of Lecture Notes in Computer Science, S. 3–17. Springer
12. Furbach U, Schon C (2018) Reasoning and consciousness. Teaching a theorem prover to let its mind wander. In The Third Conference on Artificial Intelligence and Theorem Proving, AITP2018. http://aitp-conference.org/2018/aitp18-proceedings.pdf
13. Metzinger T (2001) Postbiotisches Bewußtsein: Wie man ein künstliches Subjekt baut und warum wir es nicht tun sollten. Computer. Gehirn. Was kann der Mensch? Was können die Computer?
14. Furbach U, Glöckner I, Pelzer B (2010) An application of automated reasoning in natural language question answering. AI Commun 23(2–3):241–265
15. Metzinger T (2007) Self models. Scholarpedia 2(10):4174

12

Language

Abstract The treatment of language plays a central role in AI. Language is one of the means of expression that distinguishes humans to a special degree. The historical view of language is being replaced by modern linguistics. It examines in particular language as a sign system, language ability (competence) and speech (performance). All sub-areas can be found in varying degrees in computer science and AI.

"Cäcilia" is written on the tourist ship, illuminated by the morning sun, which sails along the Rhine and calls at places of interest. Every ship has a name by which it is identified. It perhaps refers to an affinity the owner has with a person bearing that name, or wishes for the ship (Esperanza). I immediately think of Sister Cecilia when I think of "Cecilia," who taught me in the third grade of elementary school. The name of the patroness of church music suited her because she could sing and play the piano well herself. She told us children that she was married to Jesus, which alienated me greatly at the time. I also didn't know at the time that St. Cecilia was a passionate virgin, had promised herself to Jesus Christ according to tradition, and had Josephite marriage with her husband. While I was pondering her name, "Cecilia" had already moved on quite a bit.

Not every name, not every word makes me wonder. Most of the time we communicate as if the terms and phrases were equally familiar to us. Where would we get if we were to examine every expression for its connotations — be they biographical or cognitive? Even the grammatical use of words generally succeeds without linguistic pre-considerations. Young children use singular and plural, inflect verbs,

© The Author(s), under exclusive license to Springer Fachmedien Wiesbaden GmbH, part of Springer Nature 2023

U. Barthelmeß, U. Furbach, *A Different Look at Artificial Intelligence*,
https://doi.org/10.1007/978-3-658-38474-6_12

put words in the right order without knowing what sentence members or parts of speech are. They become acquainted with grammar and its technical language later in school and use it to learn foreign languages. When acquiring their mother tongue, they imitate speech patterns of experienced speakers, intuitively grasp the laws of construction and leave the fine-tuning to the corrective intervention of competent speakers. There are also adults who are not particularly familiar with language rules and yet are able to implement them. Often the speech situation helps: the world referred to by the sender (i.e. the speaker) is within reach, there is prior knowledge of the subject matter, the receiver's antennae are tuned to readiness to understand; he too knows the context, grasps the message and possibly also the sender's subliminal message, his feelings, attitudes, expectations, and so on. This works – most of the time!

Unfortunately, as we know, there are exceptions: Misunderstandings, disputes, different interpretations of sentences, wrong or fuzzy translations. Just think of many an instruction manual that is more puzzling than helpful. In advertising and political propaganda, meanings of terms are twisted to manipulate the addressees. Controversial are also neologisms, alienations of words in the youth language, which wants to distance itself from the adult language. The list could be continued at will, because linguistic systems are extremely complex, offer an infinite variety of expression possibilities, but also some construction sites.

Linguistics is constantly providing new approaches to describing these systems. Many of them are helpful and plausible, but usually capture only a subset of the phenomenon of language.

The phrase "Cäcilia treibt ab!"[1] comes to mind – who knows why. The phrase has a surface with two different possible interpretations: The captain would refer it to his ship, I think of Sister Cecilia and find pleasure in the somewhat disrespectful pun. To understand it, one has to know the meaning of the words, especially the double meaning of the verb "abtreiben", the structure of the sentences and possibly also the background of the speaker or his intention to speak.

In the following, we will first address the meaning of language in AI and then make references to linguistic or language-philosophical concepts.

12.1 Language in AI

Machine translation of natural language has been on the agenda as a research program since the founding of the field of AI. Very quickly, the field of "computational linguistics" was established in the 1950s and 1960s. However, in

---

[1] In German a homonym with meanings "to drift" and "to have an abortion".

the course of the following decades it became apparent that the task of understanding and subsequently translating texts in spoken or written form is more difficult than originally assumed. In the meantime, however, development has made immense progress: we are used to communicating with our smartphones using spoken language, and even in our living rooms we control the lighting, the stereo system or the television by voice. We will explain this development in the following.

But languages play an important role not only in AI, but also in computer science. In computer science, the central problem is how to tell a computer what tasks to perform and how to perform them – a language is needed for this communication. Very early on, the role of such "programming languages" was recognized. In AI, of course, one had similar problems, since computers were programmed here as well.

Syntax

First, we turn to computer science and programming languages. Digital computers process sequences of zeros and ones – represented by "power off" and "power on". Such sequences can represent numbers or letters. For example, the sequence 1000001 can denote the number 65 or even the letter *A*. On this basis, a computer can calculate or also process texts. But also the instructions for this processing have to be coded in the same way. Thus, the sequence 0000 0001 1101 0000 can represent the instruction to add the numbers in two specific memory locations of a computer. Now it would be extremely tedious to create complex arithmetic instructions, or "programs," in such a machine language. Instead, in the early days of computer science, people began to use languages for programming that could be used more easily by humans – so-called higher-level programming languages. However, such programs must then be translated into the machine language of zeros and ones.

The research and construction of such "translators" or "compilers" was an important field of research in computer science until the 1980s. An extremely powerful tool for this purpose was provided as early as the 1950s by the linguist Noam Chomsky. Chomsky became known for his authoritative contributions to structural linguistics and the introduction of formal and generative grammars.

On 07. 12. 1928, Noam Chomsky

is born in Philadelphia, Pennsylvania, USA, to Jewish parents. He grows up as the older of two brothers in a middle-class immigrant family in a working-class neighborhood of Philadelphia. His politically engaged mother, originally from Belarus, lays the foundation for socially critical attitudes. His Ukrainian father, a professor of Hebraic studies, encouraged his linguistic interests. In the environment of the working class, which was directly affected by the depression of the 1930s and the repression of the state, his perception of social injustice was sharpened. The rise of National Socialism makes him a victim of anti-Semitic discrimination. At the age of 16, he begins to study at the University of Pennsylvania and is particularly enthusiastic about structural linguistics. For him, the study of language was not an end in itself; he was also interested in being able to fathom the human mind more deeply. After completing his bachelor's and master's degrees, he was awarded a scholarship in 1951 to study at Harvard University, which offered him unrestricted scientific work opportunities.

There he received his doctorate in linguistics in 1955 with a dissertation that already contained the ideas for his groundbreaking work "Syntactic Structures" (1957), with which he achieved world fame. It is the outline of a theory of language, the so-called Generative Transformational Grammar. Chomsky postulated that the equations of transformational grammar could be seen as a clue to the innate construction principles of the human brain, and derived from this the thesis of a universal grammar. In contrast to the behaviourists, according to whom humans are more or less programmed by external stimuli, Chomsky's conception of man is characterised by a free and creative mind. From this he also derives that no one has the right to dominate and oppress others, and sees himself confirmed in his political actions.

From 1961 he teaches as a full professor at the Massachusetts Institute of Technology (MIT). During this time, Chomsky begins to express himself more clearly politically in public. Since 1964 he has protested against the intervention of the USA in Vietnam. In 1969, he publishes "Amerika und die neuen Mandarine", a collection of essays on the Vietnam War [1]. Chomsky takes an equally clear stand against US policy in Cuba, Haiti, East Timor, Nicaragua, in the Palestinian conflict and towards the so-called rogue states, as well as on the Gulf and Kosovo wars, the question of human rights, globalisation and the neoliberal world order.

Today, in addition to his continuing undoubted importance to linguistics, he has become one of the most important critics of U.S. foreign policy, the political world order, and the power of the mass media.

Returning to Chomsky's grammars, such grammars consist of a set of rules that allow us to derive syntactically correct sentences in natural language. A very simplified set of rules could be, for example:

$$S \rightarrow NP \; VP$$
$$VP \rightarrow V \; NP$$
$$NP \rightarrow D \; N$$
$$N \rightarrow \textit{John}$$
$$N \rightarrow \textit{ball}$$
$$V \rightarrow \textit{hit}$$
$$D \rightarrow \textit{the}$$

We have here a small formal example grammar, which we will classify below as a context-free or Chomsky-2-grammar. The first rule can be read as "a sentence S consists of a nominal phrase NP followed by a verbal phrase VP". The second rule expresses that a verbal phrase VP can be a verb V followed by another nominal phrase NP. Of course, there are many more rules for a natural language, and also similar rules like those for generating *John* or for *ball* from a noun N then of course exist much more. Our example is merely to show how such a grammar can be used to construct a sentence by repeatedly applying the rules:

$$S \rightarrow N \; VP \rightarrow \textit{John} \; VP \rightarrow \textit{John} \; V \; NP \rightarrow \textit{John} \; \textit{hit} \; NP$$
$$\rightarrow \textit{John} \; \textit{hit} \; D \; N \rightarrow \textit{John} \; \textit{hit} \; \textit{the} \; N \rightarrow \textit{John} \; \textit{hit} \; \textit{the} \; \textit{ball}$$

It can be seen that a sentence S is constructed or generated by applying rules step by step until the sentence consists only of so-called terminals, i.e. the symbols in italics.

However, such a formal grammar can not only be used to generate syntactically correct sentences, it can also be used conversely to check a sentence. Is a presented sentence correct, and what is its syntactic structure? These are questions that are also important in the context of programming languages. A programmer creates a program in a programming language, such as Java, which is very common today. To translate this program into a language that can be understood by the computer, a formal grammar for Java is used in a first step to generate the syntactic structure, i.e. the structure of the program – this step is called "parsing". This structure can then be used in further steps for the translation into the computer's machine language.

For example, the grammar rule for a loop construct in the Java language looks like this:

$$\text{WhileStatement} \rightarrow \textit{while}\,(\text{Expression})\,\text{Statement}$$

Together with other rules for expression and statement, the following small Java program part can then be generated:

```
while(i<.10){
        System.out.println(i);
        i++;}
```

Here the expression is $i < 10$, and from Statement the two statements System.out.println(i); and i++; were generated using another rule not specified here.

This piece of program now has to be translated into a language, which the machine can process, so finally sequences of zeros and ones, as we discussed at the beginning.

Remarkably, Chomsky's formal grammars also play a central role in theoretical computer science. Thus, a hierarchy of grammars can be given, which differ only in the structure of their rules. The simplest grammars are the so-called Chomsky-3-grammars or regular grammars. The above example is a so-called Chomsky-2-grammar or context-free grammar. Here the left-hand sides of each rule are such that it contains only one syntactic variable, such as S, N or VP. Here, the right-hand sides of a rule are allowed to have any form. The study of such grammars, and in particular the design of procedures that decide, for a given grammar and an arbitrary sentence or program in a programming language, whether the sentence is syntactically correct and what the syntactic structure is, are an important part in theoretical computer science. Each of these hierarchy levels can be assigned a particular procedure for syntactically checking a sentence. For example, the procedure for Chomsky-3-grammars is a so-called finite state automaton, which can be programmed very efficiently. But in exchange, the class of language defined by such grammars is quite restricted. In Chomsky-1-grammars, one can enforce that rules are only applicable if a certain context is given. For example, a rule aaSb ← aacb could only apply if there are at least two a's to the left of S and at least one b to the right. So we can formulate contexts as conditions of application in such a Chomsky-1-grammar rule. In the case of Chomsky-0-grammars, there are no conditions on the appearance of the rules – there can be any strings to the left and right of the arrow. To process such grammars, one needs Turing machines, which allow the most general form of programming. We already got to know such machines as a universal theoretical model for a computer (cf. Chap. 3). In linguistics there is still a debate about which grammar models from the Chomsky hierarchy are suitable for describing natural languages. For example, we know for sure that Chomsky-3-grammars are too weak. For many languages there is also evidence that they cannot be formalized even with context-free Chomsky-2-grammars.

Semantics of Artificial Languages

The formalization of grammar, i.e. the syntax, has also led to defining the semantics of languages on the basis of syntactic structure. For artificial languages, i.e. programming languages, this was an important step for building translators for programming languages. Suppose you write a program in a programming language; you want to run it on your computer. As mentioned at the beginning, this requires translating the program into a sequence of machine instructions, that is, sequences of zeros and ones. This machine program can then be executed to do the task you had programmed. Now, you would certainly expect that the same program, if translated and run on another computer, would behave exactly the same way and produce the same result. But in order for any translator to "understand" and translate the program in the same way, the meaning of the programming language constructs must be unambiguous and clear. To do this, one can describe the semantics of such languages in various ways using other formal languages; these can be other simpler computer languages or even the language of mathematics. This then ensures that programs are processed in exactly the way the programmer intended.[2]

We have seen that the foundations for this formal treatment of programming languages have their origins in Chomskyian structural linguistics. And, of course, computational linguists have also followed this approach: Understanding natural language through syntactic analysis using Chomsky grammars, followed by semantic analysis with translation into a meta-language describing meaning. Different logics can serve as a meta-language. Already in antiquity one of the aims of logicians was to formalize discourse and argumentation of people. Also in the phase of the development of formal symbolic logic, as we use it today, the capture of the semantics of utterances in natural language played an important role. For example, the distinction between extensional and intensional semantics goes back to Gottlob Frege (1848–1925, one of the founders of modern logic). If one considers the semantics of a statement, such as *Morning star = evening star*, then under extensional semantics one would assign the same object, namely Venus, to the two different symbols *morning star* and *evening star*, and thus the equation would have the truth

---

[2] Provided, of course, that the programmer himself knows the semantics of the programming language.

value *true*. However, if one observes the intention behind the equation, one realizes that two different concepts are meant here, the bright planet in the morning sky and the bright planet in the evening sky. So under such a reading, the above equation would be *false*.

Semantics of Natural Languages

Logic as a meta-language for the semantics of natural languages thus certainly has a long tradition in linguistics. Thus, there are also numerous proposals for particular logics to account for the peculiarities of natural language. If we now want to analyze our little example sentence from above, *John hit the ball.* not only syntactically, but semantically, and enter it for this purpose into a system developed by the Dutch computational linguist Johan Bos [2], we obtain the following predicate logic formula:

$$
\begin{vmatrix}
some(A, some(B, and(and\ (balln(A), hitu(B)), \\
some(C, and)(r1CoC45Theme(C,A), and\ (r1Theme(C,B), v1hit(C))))))))
\end{vmatrix}
$$

The formula is only meant to illustrate that even for this simple example sentence a rather complex formula is needed to describe the semantic facts. We see in the formula three quantifiers *some*, the predicates *balln*, *hitv* and two predicates with the ending *Theme*, which describe topics or events. Now, when you read the sentence *John hit the ball.* you certainly associated a lot more – you know that John refers to a male person, that a ball is round, and that John probably used some form of bat. None of this is explicitly stated, but you have immediately linked the meaning of this sentence to your general knowledge of the world, and so can understand many facets of this simple statement. General knowledge about the world is something you have acquired throughout your life. How we use it, how we activate the right relevant parts when we want to understand a sentence, is an important research topic in psychology, neuroscience and of course AI. We have already discussed in detail in Chap. 5 how this knowledge can be represented, how it can be used and activated has also been discussed in Chap. 9.

For a long time, computational linguistics and AI have been dominated by the roughly outlined approach of describing the semantics of natural language statements by translating them into a formal metalanguage. With this metalanguage, either the text can be analyzed or translated into another natural language.

Recently, extremely powerful translation programs for natural languages exist that can also be used via a web interface (e.g. from Microsoft, Google or DeepL). However, these systems do not use formal semantics for translation; rather, they learn the translation from bilingual texts. Mostly convolutional neural networks are used today, as we explained them in the context of image processing in Chap. 7. These networks are trained on very large corpora of multilingual texts, so that the system learns the correct translation without explicit knowledge of rules or grammar. As you may have red in the blurb of this book, it has been translated fully automatically from the German edition into English with the help of DeepL.[3]

For a new language, the system only needs to be trained on a new bilingual corpus – the system learns the new language "by itself". Now, it could be argued that no language understanding at all is possible by such an approach, that only learned "translation schemes" are applied to generate the translation. However, there are also related methods in linguistics to capture the semantics of a language. For example, as early as 1957, the linguist John Rupert Firth laid the foundations for "distributed semantics", namely by arguing:

You shall know a word by the company it keeps [3]

The semantics of words or concepts is determined by their proximity to other words. This proximity is determined by counting occurrences of word embeddings in large text corpus. For each word or term a vector is stored, which determines the relation to other words or terms. These vectors can be generated by various statistical methods or, as mentioned above, learned by neural networks. We will now take a look at the theories of linguists and discover some analogies.

12.2   Theories of Language in Linguistics

With the "Cours de linguistique générale" [4] by Ferdinand de Saussure from 1916, modern linguistics begins and replaces historical-comparative linguistics: For Humboldt, the most prominent representative of this discipline, the objects of our perception are not things in themselves, but always only appearances (see Kant). Accordingly, perception takes place through concepts and thus makes thinking possible in the first place. Reality is created through language. Language and thinking are one for him and, since languages are different, the thinking of peoples is also different. Humboldt attempts to

---

[3] www.deepl.com retrieved on 13.8.2018.

grasp the essence of languages on the basis of their structures and, in elaborate investigations, draws up a typology of languages which classifies languages as analytical and synthetic according to their structural patterns. Analytic languages regulate syntactic tasks mainly through positional rules and unbound function words (for example, prepositions), while synthetic languages tend to use endings (affixes) for this purpose. German, for example, is a hybrid language that is currently moving from the synthetic structure to the analytic one. One example is the dwindling genitive: instead of "des Vaters", one hears more and more often "von dem Vater" (instead of the genitive of the noun one prefers the use of preposition and dative, which is perceived as simpler). – Many languages are hybrids, but some are also purely analytic or synthetic. Humboldt discovered that most Indo-European languages have a tendency to inflect, that is, they are synthetic languages. Because he associated language with worldview and assumed that inflectional languages testified to an upward evolution of the human mind, nineteenth-century language typology fell into disrepute as unscientific because of its subjective evaluation of languages.

A new ideal of science, positivism, based on the natural sciences, asserts itself and demands that only what is directly perceived – facts or sensory perceptions – is a secure basis for knowledge. The scientific ideal of objectivity and exactness prevails. In psychology, this leads to the emergence of behaviorism (from about 1910–1960), which replaces the study of the soul or mind with the study of observable human behavior.

De Saussure is therefore concerned with language as something concrete and real and examines the material of the existing, observable sound and written images. In the "Cours de linguistique générale" he formulates fundamental linguistic principles and distinguishes the following three aspects: The speech act of the individual, which is bound to his individual preconditions and is factually observable, he calls "parole". It is the personally shaped implementation of the language system, the "langue", which is available to a collective. This is based on linguistic conventions established by the use of language. These are, for example, individual languages such as English or German, but also phonetic or sign language. Langue and parole stand in a relationship of mutual conditionality, since they influence each other. It is to man's ability to speak at all that he refers with the term "langage".

In the following sections, we will discuss these three aspects.

La langue: Language as a System of Signs

La langue as a sign system is for Saussure the main object of linguistics. He formulates the fundamental properties of linguistic systems. Here are the most important ones:

Signifier and signified are the two sides of a linguistic sign. The signifier is the expression or sound side, for example "dog". The signifier is the corresponding animal that is imagined.

The arbitrariness of signs means that there is no internal correlation between expression and content. An exception are onomatopoeias, for example, the word cuckoo is related to the sound the bird makes.

In contrast to the signifier, the signified has a *linear structure,* i.e. a sequence of sounds or letters.

Syntagmatic and paradigmatic relations exist between the units of a language system:

Syntagma: The baker + bakes + the bread.
Paradigm: bakes/slices/sells;

There is a *synchronic and diachronic* view of language. The former deals with a static state of language, the latter with language change.

With these fundamental statements de Saussure founded the structuralism of linguistics. There is a multitude of variations of it, different orientations and emphases, which we will not go into in detail.

Le langage: The Faculty of Speech

De Saussure's main focus was on langue, the system of signs in a given language that enables speakers of that language to communicate.

Chomsky, on the other hand, explores the question of how it is that all people in the world can speak and communicate at all. He is not concerned with a single particular language; for him, the languages of the world are only "variations on a single theme" [5].

He is mainly concerned with the faculty of language, which de Saussure calls langage. Language is a phenomenon of life and thus a mental property of man that enables him to express an infinite number of thoughts with the help of the finite means that form the linguistic system. He calls this ability grammatical competence, which is equally inherent in the human species despite the different languages and the different cultures.

So all people have – on a deeper level – something in common. The theory of universal grammar is based on this assumption. This involves two assumptions, namely that all languages follow the same grammatical principles and that this ability to recognise and use these very principles is genetically anchored.

These principles explain how combining a limited number of words and rules can produce an unlimited number of sentences. The endless number of possible sentences is based on embedding one phrase within another phrase of the same type – this is the structural principle of recursion. In this process, phrases can be concatenated (He knows that she thinks that …) or nested (That is the hammer with which he hammered the nail on which the picture was hung that …).

The term competence refers to the general human ability to generate and understand an infinite number of linguistic expressions and to assign a structure to these expressions. The individual realization of competence, which the individual speaker performs and which may be faulty or incomplete, is called performance.

A further distinction is important: language in the sense of structure-generating grammatical competence is called I-language (I from "internalized"), it is represented in the individual as a component of the human mind. E-language (E from "externalized"), the external observable language behavior, represents the totality of utterances that can be made in a language community.

According to this division, there are E-language and I-language linguistics. The E-language linguist collects extensive language samples, so-called corpora, and then describes their properties. Based on the regularities of these language samples, he creates a grammar.

The I-language linguist, on the other hand, views language as an internal property of the human mind rather than something external. Language is conceived as a system represented in the mind, that is, in the brain of a single individual. His grammar describes the intuitive knowledge of language rather than the sentences produced on its basis. Chomsky's theoretical approaches belong to the tradition of I-language research.

There are also two tendencies in language teaching: Those teachers who favor E-language methods and emphasize communication and behavior, and those who favor I-language methods and emphasize language knowledge (e.g., grammar rules).

Computational linguists can also be roughly divided into two camps: those who analyze huge amounts of language data (corpus linguists), and those who write rules. In the previous section on the semantics of natural languages, this very distinction was also made: Semantics is defined in a meta-language – logic, for example – by following grammar rules, or by ignoring these rules and analyzing huge corpora of texts. The analysis can be done with statistical means or with adaptive neural networks.

The concept of universal grammar is controversial. Its existence is contested again and again – especially by behaviourists – who regard language acquisition exclusively as the result of a learning process.

The theory of universal grammar has recently been supported by cognitive brain research: In 2018, the neuropsychologist Angela Friederici presented the first empirical evidence pointing to the existence of an organ responsible for universal grammar. This is said to be a bundle of fibers in the brain between Broca's area and Wernicke's area [6]. Broca's area is responsible for grammar, Wernicke's area for words. A particular nerve fiber bundle that connects the two areas is responsible for the rules that combine words. In monkeys, this connection is very weak and not yet fully functional in newborn infants. Further empirical studies are still pending.

La Parole: The Speaking

The theories discussed so far more or less exclude one factor of languages: the speaking person in life. In de Saussure's case, this factor is recorded at the level of parole, and in Chomsky's at the level of performance, but it is treated rather stepmotherly. Yet language exists because people speak, and not as an end in itself. Man as a living being who has to get along in the world communicates through language.

Paul Valéry (1871–1945), a renowned French lyricist, philosopher and essayist wrote, that any philosophical system in which the body of man does not play a fundamental role is stupid and useless. Knowledge has the body of man as its limit [7].

With this in mind, we turn to a view of language that focuses on the human being as a bodily being. We will first consider considerations inspired by Merleau Ponty's theory of the body and present aspects of "Sprache als leibliche Gebärde" – the title of the highly readable and insightful dissertation by Lilianne Grams [8] – to which we first refer. Subsequently, we address language models that foreground humans as speaking subjects.

As already explained above in the chapter on consciousness, the human body assumes a central significance in the phenomenological way of thinking. As the existential core of our life, it gives it meaning and is the expression of the speaker's intentionality. It is the medium of our expressions and gives them meaning, among other things through language.

Language is the culmination and limit of the expressive capacity of the body, which articulates itself in various ways. Gestures, extralinguistic phenomena such as laughing and crying, paralinguistic phenomena such as voice pitch, rhythm, silence, stagnation have an important communicative value, since they show how the speaking subject feels. The synchrony of gesture or the corresponding paralinguistic phenomena and speech in the speech act points to the relationship of meaning between gesture and speech, the cooperation of bodily movements with what is said underlines the statement and intention of the speaker.

Verbal expression and gesture find their counterpart in the habitual and current body: The habitual body is the totality of the experiences of the human being in his autobiographical history, his hereditary dispositions, his constitution, his temperament and character. The current body updates the habitual body so that it is never static and grows.

Accordingly, there are two manifestations in verbal utterance, namely spoken language and speaking language. The spoken language (instituted language/language as past, comparable to langue) corresponds to the habitual body, it provides objectified knowledge, so that the conceptual sense always seems to be clearly given. In contrast, the speaking language (analogous to the parole), the counterpart of the present body, that is, the present language in the making, generates meaning only through language; it contains a dynamic moment. A clear distinction between spoken language and speaking language is therefore not possible, since the two are mutually dependent. Acquired meanings, too, must once have been new meanings.

In gesture, too, two forms of appearance are to be distinguished: instituted gesture and the original spontaneous gesture. The former – like spoken language – has acquired universal validity as a sign function. It conveys cognitive content, for example nodding as an affirmation, raising one's hand at auctions, etc. The spontaneous gesture is to be seen as the immediate realisation of a mental content. In the execution of the gesture the subject experiences his emotional intentions. The gesture is not a shell of the sensations, but realizes them. Let us take anger as an example: we clench our fists, hit the table, stamp our foot. When we speak, we are loud, speak faster and higher. All these extra- and paralinguistic expressions are the realization of anger.[4] The psychic content cannot be separated from the physical form; they are poles of a unity. So language and gesture are in the body. How do they get there?

The consciousness of the subject is in a factual situation. It first experiences subliminal intentions that are translated into formulable meanings and expresses this through gesture or verbal expression. The body transcends itself by means of language or gesture. After language acquisition, language or gesture in the speaker is part of his bodily equipment. This explains the synchrony of speech and gesture in the speech act mentioned above. Also, speech and gesture are equally immediate and spontaneous, but not arbitrary, since the speaker is guided by intentions. There is an original silence (unspoken

---

[4] The popular, sometimes inflationary use of emojis in digital communication may stem from the urge to let the body speak.

thoughts, existential trigger, surplus of meaning) that is broken by gesture and word. Language must be integrated, literally incorporated, by the speaker through a process of appropriation. After language acquisition, language is in the speaker. It is part of his body. An example in this regard is easy to follow: If one has forgotten a word, neither the paraphrased meaning nor the concrete conception of the object is of any use; one tries to approach it in its sound and articulation: One can, for example, recall the alphabet and see if certain sounds signal the buried presence of a word or name. Often the word or name presents itself to the memory like a summoned spirit. Perhaps in this way different regions in the brain are brought into connection by synchronizing their oscillation (see Chap. 9) – this would be a vivid confirmation of the thesis that language belongs to the body of the speaker.

Unlike the gesture, which the subject does not normally see, every verbal utterance is heard and thus reflection is switched on. In the speech act, both the thinking and the speaking subject become active. A creative performance of the speaker consists in realizing a "wild" unformulated thought by choosing an adequate mode of expression on the basis of the available word meanings. The structures of spoken language are thus open, and the speaking subject shapes and transforms them as he uses them. Thus language remains in motion. The speaking subject is the language he speaks. The word acquires its clear meaning only when it is spoken.

Just as the gesture says more than what it represents – a handshake as a touch of flesh and bone means turning towards the other, the greeted –, language leaves its actual appearance (phonetic sounds, syntax) behind and refers to the statement.

The considerations on the gestural meaning of speech lead directly to the speech act theory, whose genesis and most important statements we will briefly touch upon here [9].

The term speech act was first used by Karl Bühler (1879–1963); he conceives of language as a tool (organon) intended to achieve certain goals in communication. He calls the use of language in a concrete situation speech action, not only as an actualization of language (see performance in Chomsky), but also in the sense of a social action. Ludwig Wittgenstein (1889–1951) states in his "Philosophischen Untersuchungen" [10] that in order to understand the meaning of a word, one must pay attention to its use, that is, to what someone does when he uses a certain word. By the term "language games" he means forms of use of language: "Das Wort 'Sprachspiel' soll hier hervorheben, daß das Sprechen der Sprache ein Teil ist einer Tätigkeit, oder einer Lebensform. (...) Befehlen, und nach Befehlen handeln; – Beschreiben eines Gegenstands nach dem Ansehen, oder nach

Messungen; Herstellen eines Gegenstands nach einer Beschreibung (Zeichnung); Berichten eines Hergangs; (...)."[5]

These kinds of verbs, called language games, are central to the two main proponents of speech act theory, the American philosophers of language Austin and his student Searle. For simplicity, we present Searle's theory, which does not differ significantly from Austin's: Two considerations stand in the foreground, the meaning of linguistic signs is derived from their use, and speaking is acting. The following levels can be distinguished in a speech act: On the first level is the act of utterance, that is, a speaker expresses himself according to the rules of phonology and grammar. On the next level, his reference to certain objects in the world is recorded (propositional act). A third level is acting by speaking, for example, asking, commanding (illocutionary act). The last level concerns the influence a speaker exerts on the receiver (perlocutionary act). Acts of the lower levels cannot be performed by themselves, but are only components or aspects of an act of the respective higher level.

It goes without saying that level three in particular is of interest to speech act theorists. The intentions of the real speaker, the concrete communicative intentions of action, are in the foreground and are of vital interest to him.

Speech Act Theory and AI

Now, speech act theory is not only relevant for linguists; there are also many possible applications in AI. Take, for example, environments where robots cooperate with humans. As a common example, one might imagine a kitchen where a human and a robot work together. Here, level two, the reference to specific objects in the kitchen, will certainly play an important role. But only if all four levels are equally considered, a good and efficient communication and cooperation can take place. Even if we consider robots alone and assume that several robots should cooperate, speech act theory offers important approaches. In such "multi-agent systems", communication and cooperation must of course take place in the same way. In fact, the so-called BDI approach has become established there, which was significantly influenced by speech act theory. BDI is an abbreviation for "belief, desire and intention", where aspects of levels two and four are clearly addressed. Such BDI architectures are used in various multi-agent systems, for example in robot soccer, where

---

[5] The word 'language game' is here meant to emphasize that the speaking of language is a part of an activity, or a form of life. (...) Commanding, and acting according to commands; – describing an object according to appearance, or according to measurements; making an object according to a description (drawing); reporting a course of events; (...).".

autonomous robots are supposed to cooperate without having negotiated precise plans beforehand. Football has to be played fast, situation-dependent and still cooperative. This requires communication, where, however, the act of utterance according to level one is less important.

12.3 Summary

We have only been able to address a few subfields of linguistics here and see that there are many facets that are also relevant in AI. In particular, the distinction between corpus-based and rule-based approaches can be found in both fields. Corpus-based approaches are also often referred to as statistical methods and are very often used together with learning neural networks. In language theory, the speaking human being standing in life is also taken into account, and it is precisely these approaches that can also be important when dealing with autonomous intelligent agents, as we have seen in the example of BDI architectures.

References

1. Chomsky N (1969) Amerika und die neuen Mandarine: politische und zeitgeschichtliche Essays. Suhrkamp, Frankfurt
2. Bos J (2008) Wide-coverage semantic analysis with boxer. In: Proceedings of the 2008 conference on semantics in text processing, STEP '08, S. 277–286. Association for Computational Linguistics, Stroudsburg, PA, USA
3. Firth JR (1991) Papers in linguistics 1934–1951: Rep. Oxford University Press, Oxford
4. de Saussure F (1916) Cours de linguistique générale. Edition critique préparée par Tullio de Mauro, Payot
5. Chomsky N (2000) New horizons in the study of language and mind. Cambridge University Press, New York
6. Friederici A, Kara S (2018) Ich denke, dass er denkt, dass ... https://www.zeit.de/2018/18/universalgrammatik-sprache-kinder-gehirn-neuropsychologie. Accessed 4 Nov 2018
7. Valéry P (2011) Ich grase meine Gehirnwiese ab. Paul Valéry und seine verborgenen Cahiers. Eichborn, Frankfurt a. M.
8. Grams L (1978) Sprache als leibliche Gebärde. PhD thesis, LMU
9. Wikipedia (2018) Sprechakttheorie – Wikipedia, Die freie Enzyklopädie [Online; Stand 7. November 2018]
10. Wittgenstein L (2001) Philosophische Untersuchungen. Kritisch-genetische Edition. Wissenschaftliche Buchgesellschaft, Darmstadt

13

Epilogue

Abstract This concluding chapter takes a critical look back at the themes of this book. In particular, the need for explainable AI is postulated.

In the course of our work, a parable has come to mind that vividly illustrates how difficult, if not hopeless, our endeavor is to track down natural and artificial memory, its modes of functioning and articulation. Where to start, what to focus on, what to leave out? There are so many aspects, approaches and insights! Here is one of the many versions of the story, which is said to be at least 3000 years old:

13.1 The Blind and the Elephant

A king sent five blind scholars on a journey. They were to find out what an elephant was. When they returned, they were to report back to him. The first scholar had touched the elephant's trunk and said, "An elephant is like a snake." The second, who had touched the tusk, replied, "An elephant is like a spear." The third had felt the ear and said, "An elephant is like a fan." The fourth said, "But no, an elephant is like a pillar." He had touched one leg of the elephant. The last, who had grabbed the elephant by the tail, spoke, "An elephant is like a rope." They could not agree and argued bitterly with each other.

© The Author(s), under exclusive license to Springer Fachmedien Wiesbaden GmbH, part of Springer Nature 2023
U. Barthelmeß, U. Furbach, *A Different Look at Artificial Intelligence*, https://doi.org/10.1007/978-3-658-38474-6_13

We are miles away from describing the elephant, if it is possible at all. However, we have found that the parts we have addressed are often not so dissimilar in both the natural and artificial elephant. This may well be due to the fact that the natural being, the human, manufactures the artificial one, the AI, and takes its cue from its own image, which is actually obvious. Can he do otherwise at all?

In AI, this aspect is often taken into account by the division into strong and weak AI. We already described in Chap. 2 that strong AI takes humans as a model and tries to model their approach and their ability as well as possible in the artificial system. Weak AI, on the other hand, is to be understood more as an engineering approach – the main thing is that the system has the function, how it comes about is irrelevant.

In various contexts we have seen machine learning techniques, especially those based on artificial neural networks, being used very successfully. Now, one might think that these are methods of strong AI, since after all, the neural network of humans is being modeled and even the learning in such artificial networks is modeled after the natural one. Take vision as an example, we have discussed that AI systems are able to classify objects in images at least as well as humans. However, if you ask such a system why it recognized and classified, for example, a cat in an image as a cat, you cannot currently get a statement. A human would probably argue that the fur, ears, eyes and size indicate a cat, but that's exactly what the AI system can't do. In the neural network, there are a large number of numbers that stand at the edges of the network as a result of the learning process – but why these stand for a cat or precisely what is typical about a cat image cannot be deduced from this. The same is true for many other applications of machine learning. The success of some applications is very impressive, and they have found their way into everyday life and onto the market. The more these techniques influence our everyday life, the stronger the demand for explainable AI becomes. AI systems should therefore be able to justify their decisions in a way that we humans can understand. This is particularly important in areas where humans and AI systems cooperate; here, explainable AI could lead to trusting cooperation. Now, one could argue that humans often construct reasons for their decisions only retrospectively; recognizing a cat in a picture happens quite spontaneously, only asked afterwards do we construct the essential properties of a cat's image. But such a retrospective explanation could also be desirable for an AI system, for example, if an autonomous vehicle is involved in an accident, it may well be important for the administration of justice or for the investigation of an insurance claim to learn reasons for the decisions of the autonomous vehicle.

We have attempted to show a small step in the direction of explainable AI by showing parallels between AI methods and other disciplines in the humanities and natural sciences through various examples. These similarities certainly need to be further explored and developed; we believe it could be rewarding for all sides.

Printed in the United States
by Baker & Taylor Publisher Services

Printed in the United States
by Baker & Taylor Publisher Services